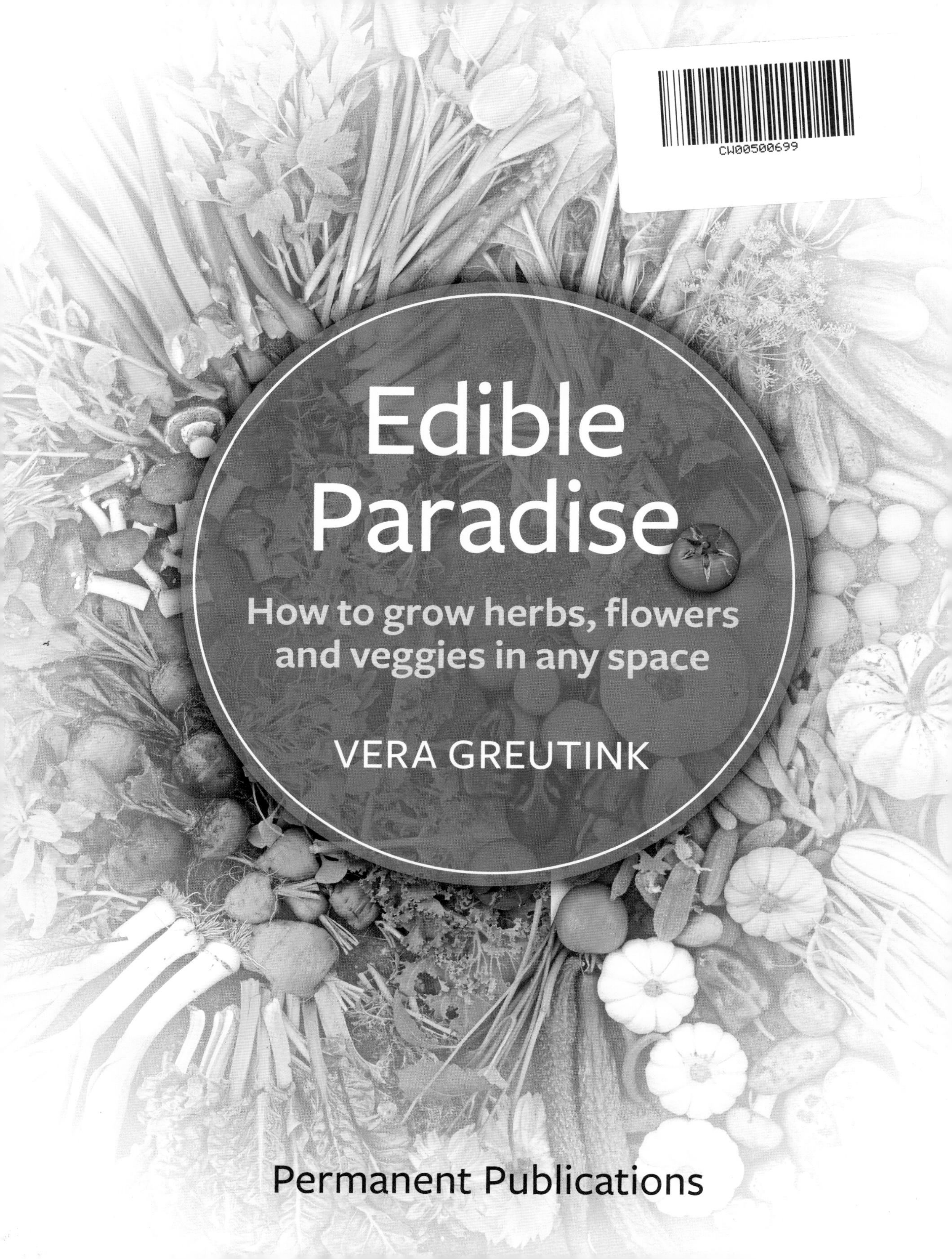

Edible Paradise

How to grow herbs, flowers and veggies in any space

VERA GREUTINK

Permanent Publications

Published by
Permanent Publications
Hyden House Ltd
The Sustainability Centre
East Meon
Hampshire GU32 1HR
United Kingdom
Tel: 01730 823 311
International code: +44 (0)
Email: enquiries@permaculture.co.uk
Web: www.permanentpublications.co.uk

Distributed in the USA by
Chelsea Green Publishing Company, PO Box 428, White River Junction, VT 05001
www.chelseagreen.com

Photography by Remco Greutink and Vera Greutink

Designed by Two Plus George Limited, info@twoplusgeorge.co.uk

Printed in the UK by Bell & Bain, Thornliebank, Glasgow

MIX Paper from responsible sources FSC www.fsc.org FSC® C007785

All paper from FSC certified mixed sources.
The Forest Stewardship Council (FSC) is a non-profit international organisation established to promote the responsible management of the world's forests.

Products carrying the FSC label are independently certified to assure consumers that they come from forests that are managed to meet the social, economic and ecological needs of present and future generations.

British Library Cataloguing-in-Publication Data
A catalogue record for this book is available from the British Library

ISBN 978 1 85623 325 5

Praise for the book

Vera Greutink covers some really valuable fresh ground in this book. I am impressed by her insight and experience, especially in the area of annual polycultures. These are one of the central features of the book, not only in outside beds but also polycultures in pots for those who have a more limited space for growing, and have rarely been embraced to this degree in other books. I recommend it to all food growers.

Martin Crawford, author and founder of the Agroforestry Research Trust

Whether your patch is an allotment, community garden, back yard or even just a patio or balcony, this gorgeous book is packed with information and inspiration, empowering anybody to create productive and beautiful regenerative edible landscapes today.

Graham Burnett, permaculture teacher and author of *The Vegan Book of Permaculture*

This is a real permaculture gardener's bible! It's wonderful to have such a comprehensive gardening book written from a permaculture perspective. Vera Greutink writes with the clarity of her great experience of working with plants in many different situations. She demystifies some permaculture practices which new gardeners or traditional gardeners can find intimidating or confusing. She considers the many different situations of the grower and lays out basic principles and practical methods to make growing healthy food in harmony with nature accessible to all. This is a brilliant companion for new or experienced gardeners and I will add it to my list of recommended reading for gardening and permaculture students, alongside those which inspired Vera to develop her own green fingers.

Caroline Aitken, permaculture teacher, designer and author of *Food from your Forest Garden*

Vera Greutink, editor of the magazine *De Tuin op Tafel* (The Garden on the Table) in the Netherlands, brings her practical experience to this welcome book. Beautifully illustrated it's a great text to encourage the less experienced aspirant to growing their own. It focusses on the reality of most European gardeners, which is to be working on small plots often in urban situations and proposes workable solutions for these challenges in a clear and succinct way. The chapter on herbs is a clear test of knowledge which she passes with flying colours. She is well connected into all the environmental issues and seasonality. Her advice on what to do when is exemplary. I wish this book every success. If only mainstream Dutch agriculture would listen to these lessons!

Graham Bell, internationally renowned speaker, teacher and author on Permaculture, Forest Gardening and growing your own food

Such a useful book about an area of gardening that really deserves greater exploration. Edible Paradises are the future!

Lia Leendertz, garden and cookery writer and author of *The Almanac: a Seasonal Guide*

Within seconds of finding Vera's YouTube gardening channel 'GrownToCook' I knew I found something very special. Her garden is not only amazingly bountiful; it's also beautiful. And she achieves her results using an approach that is environmentally friendly and low effort. Now, with *Edible Paradise*, readers can benefit from Vera's many years of experience, and learn, step by step, how to apply her methods to grow a bountiful and beautiful garden of their own. Whether you're growing in containers, your backyard, or a community garden, *Edible Paradise* will help you achieve your gardening goals.

Partick Dolan, OneYardRevolution

One quick glance at Vera's Instagram page will completely back up why this book is called *Edible Paradise*. That is exactly what she has created on her abundant ¼ acre plot in the Netherlands. *Edible Paradise* is a goldmine of knowledge and inspiration for any gardener, with Vera's voice clearly guiding you through the creativity of growing your own delicious food. It is so refreshing to see the importance of soil health playing a vital role throughout, something which many gardening books fail to fully respect. This book will influence the way you grow food forever, take my word for it.

Huw Richards, YouTuber, gardener and author of *Veg in One Bed*

Contents

PART 1
Container Gardening

PART 2

The Permaculture Kitchen Garden

Introduction

Dear (future) gardener,

Lest you think that 'green fingers' are something you either are born with, or will never possess, let me tell you that my first garden (which I had at the ripe age of 12), was a complete failure. But I believe that gardening, like anything else, is a matter of practice, fuelled by keen interest and the determination to try again if you fail. I kept gardening and each successive garden was better and more productive than the one before and I'm sure the same is possible for you.

My approach to gardening was enhanced when in 1999 I discovered permaculture, a design framework inspired by natural ecosystems. But while there were plenty of books explaining the principles and design techniques, they often concentrated on creating perennial systems and I could find little about how to put these into practice in the kitchen garden. For example, even though annual polycultures sounded like a great idea, I could find few concrete examples beyond the well-known three sisters.

In the years since, I've been experimenting with the permaculture techniques in any garden I had access to – in our community garden, on my parents' plot and in my own gardens. What you now have in front of you is all the knowledge I've gathered along the way.

I believe in small-scale solutions, in starting where you are and doing your best there. Instead of wishing for an acre plot where you could realise dreams of self-sufficiency, make the best possible use of your balcony. Any bunch of herbs that you grow yourself and that has not been sprayed, packaged and transported, is a small win. Which is why my book starts with exploring and maximising the possibilities of growing in containers and then moves on to growing in garden soil. I take you through all the steps, from choosing a site, removing weeds without digging, to designing the plot to function as best it can for you and filling it with a variety of produce so that you can enjoy harvests from it all year long. I also believe that beauty and productivity are not mutually exclusive and that the garden you'll create can be just as nice to look at as any ornamental planting.

My hope is that wherever you find yourself on your gardening journey, whether you're a complete beginner or a seasoned veteran, this book will provide you with inspiration and practical steps that will not only make your gardening life easier and more enjoyable, but will also improve the soil you are tending and contribute to the diversity in your area.

Happy gardening,
Vera

About the Author

Vera Greutink is a permaculture gardener, teacher and designer based in the Netherlands. She's been gardening for over 30 years during which she has created many beautiful and productive gardens. Vera regularly contributes to Dutch and Belgian gardening magazines as well as the English *Permaculture Magazine*. She is also Editor in Chief of the edible gardening magazine, *De Tuin op Tafel* (The Garden on the Table). To see what's new at her ¼ acre permaculture plot, you can follow her on Instagram and on YouTube (both as GrownToCook).

Acknowledgements

Every gardening book builds upon a long and rich tradition of garden writing and I am immensely indebted to many gardeners who have shared their experiences before me, among many others: Eliot Coleman and Barbara Damrosch (particularly for their writing on winter growing), Charles Dowding (for his work on no-dig gardening), Joy Larkcom and Rosalind Creasy (for their enthusiasm for edible landscaping), Peter Bauwens (who has introduced me to many wonderful new varieties) and Sarah Raven (who has inspired me to start growing flowers for cutting). I have also been influenced by many permaculture gardeners/designers, in particular: David Holmgren, Patrick Whitefield, Toby Hemenway and Fransjan de Waard.

In recent years the generous gardening community on both YouTube and Instagram has been a great source of inspiration and knowledge – I am especially thankful to the gardeners who tried one of my polycultures and shared with me how it did in their climate.

My friend Marina kindly volunteered to be my first reader, checking my grammar and making sure my book was understandable even to non-gardeners.

The book would not have seen the light of day without the team at Permanent Publications, especially Maddy, Tim and Rozie who believed in it from the beginning and have been kind and patient throughout the process of creating this book.

I am thankful to my parents and my sister, who always cheer me on, share my love of homegrown food and foraging and do not mind me conducting experiments in their gardens.

Romeo, our honorary godson and the only teenager we know who is interested in gardening, has helped with many a project over the years.

My children Esther and Sebastiaan are not gardeners (yet) but appreciate the effort I put into feeding them 'real food' and are a big part of why I grow fruits and vegetables in the first place.

But the biggest 'thank you' is for my husband Remco, who's been gardening with me for over 15 years, has taken most of the photographs in this book, is still prepared to try anything I have grown and cooked, and keeps his good cheer even when mine wavers.

part 1
Growing in Containers

If you are a gardener without access to soil, and all the growing space you have is a windowsill, a balcony, or, for the lucky few, a rooftop terrace, growing in containers is likely your only option. But it can also be a solution if you know or suspect that the soil in your garden is contaminated and unsuitable for growing edibles. I am a gardener blessed with a fairly large garden and healthy soil, but I too have a cheerful collection of miscellaneous containers close to my back door. They are decorative and bring the garden a little closer to the house, making a bridge between the inside and the outside. Furthermore, they make it easy to accommodate specific plant requirements. For example, I can make an alkaline potting mix for lavender or rosemary, or an acidic one if I want to grow blueberries. Containers are mobile which means moderately hardy plants grown in containers can be brought inside when temperatures drop. For many years, we grew two beautiful fig plants, 'Pingo de Mel' and 'Petite Negri', in large containers. During the summer months they adorned our terrace and for the winter, we moved them into our unheated shed to shelter them from freezing winds. In a container I could provide them with the well-drained, alkaline soil they needed and because their roots were restricted by the size of the container, the plants matured faster and bore fruits early.

Compared to plants grown outside in the garden soil, container grown vegetables, herbs and fruit will require much more attention and care. You'll have to carefully monitor their needs, watering and feeding as needed. You can perceive this as a necessary evil or choose to see the time you spend taking care of your little garden as an opportunity to slow down and be mindful, connecting with a piece of nature amidst the city.

CHAPTER 1

The Basics

Pots and containers

You can buy pots and containers designated for growing plants but you can also re-purpose all kinds of objects into planters. A zealous container gardener looks at any object as a potential plant container and will turn anything from a wine barrel to a trashcan to a toilet pot into a planter. The aesthetics of the container garden are of course entirely up to you, but it is good to be aware of a few practical points.

Most store-bought containers are either plastic or ceramic. Plastic containers are lighter and therefore easier to move around. If you garden on a balcony or a roof, the weight of a container is an important consideration and lightweight containers are probably a better choice. Of course, weight is also what ensures stability and lightweight containers on a windy roof need to be secured so that they do not get knocked over by wind. Water does not permeate through plastic, which means your pots will not dry out as quickly, but it also means that you need to water carefully in order to prevent the potting soil from getting waterlogged.

Terracotta pots look classy but because they are porous, water will evaporate more quickly and you will need to water them more frequently. They are best suited for plants that hate being waterlogged, such as Mediterranean herbs. Most terracotta pots (except the most expensive ones made out of high quality clay and fired at high temperatures) can crack when they freeze and should not be left outside during the winter months. Glazed ceramic containers are usually more robust and not porous, so water will not evaporate as quickly.

Wooden containers are prone to rot (hardwood ones less so than softwood). A preservative will prolong their lifespan, but obviously it must be non-toxic, especially if you are planning to grow edibles. Metal containers are long lasting but can heat up excessively if they are in a sunny spot. This can be beneficial for some heat-loving crops (peppers, aubergines) but can be fatal for fruit trees in winter. If the pot heats up on a sunny day, the tree thinks it's spring and starts to produce sugar. But because the plant is not actively growing at that moment, the sugar is not used and turns into alcohol, which can kill the plant. To prevent this you can either move the container into the shade for the winter or wrap the container in something like a reed mat.

My own container garden consists of a large zinc tub plus multiple blue-glazed ceramic pots and a few terracotta ones that I have collected from mainly second-hand stores and flea markets over the years. The colour blue ties my little container garden together even though the containers come in many different shapes and sizes and are filled with a highly varied collection of plants.

Potting soil

The ideal potting mix is moisture-retentive, well aerated and well structured. Ordinary garden soil will not do because it quickly becomes compacted as a result of frequent watering and also because it usually harbours weed seeds as well as potential pests. Commercially available potting composts are either soil-based or peat-based. Soil- or loam-based mixes are good at retaining moisture and nutrients but are also heavier, which might be an issue on a balcony or a roof. They are best suited for plants that will grow in the container for multiple seasons such as (small) fruit trees and fruiting bushes. Loam-less potting mixes are either based on peat or a peat substitute such as coconut coir or fine bark. Neither peat nor its substitutes are rich in nutrients and the primary reason behind their use as a growing medium is their capacity to retain water. However, once peat dries out, it will not easily become moist again. Water will simply run through the dried out peat and the only solution is usually to submerge the whole container in water until the potting mix gets saturated again. From an environmental point of view, the use of peat as a growing medium is more than problematic – mining for peat destroys the rich biodiversity of peat bogs and unlocks the carbon that was stored there, contributing to the greenhouse effect. And even though peat is technically a renewable resource, it needs specific circumstances and centuries of time to be created. For this reason, bark or coconut coir (the processed fibre extracted from coconut husk) are better alternatives.

If you have the space and time to make leafmould (well-composted leaves of deciduous trees and shrubs), it too makes a good base for a potting mix. Depending on what tree the leaves come from, it will take about two years for them to break down into a dark and crumbly leafmould. The leafmould can then be mixed with equal parts of loam, grit and garden compost (or well-rotted manure) and used for perennial plants.

For annual plants that will only need the potting mix for (a part of) a growing season, I use a mix of three parts coconut coir, one part homemade worm compost and one part sand (or vermiculite). If I have it to hand, I also like to add a bit (just about 2%) of bentonite, a clay mineral that will improve the retention of water and nutrients. For plants such as Mediterranean herbs or figs that prefer alkaline soil, I add about half a cup of lime per wheelbarrow of the mix.

This potting mix can be recycled and reused the following season, provided you add new nutrients. I usually empty my pots into a wheelbarrow and mix in about 25% fresh homemade (worm) compost and some vermiculite if it looks like the mix needs to be aerated. This will work for a few seasons in a row, after which I will start with a fresh mix.

Watering and feeding

Container plants are like kids incapable of growing up – they will forever need your care. You have to feed them and make sure they have enough to drink (but it must not be too much either), and that they get enough sunlight (but do not burn). In short, if you want your plants to thrive, you'll have to keep coddling them.

While plants growing outside in the garden will get the majority of water they need from the skies, when it comes to container plants, watering is your responsibility. During the summer months that means watering daily, even twice a day in hot weather. The best water for plants is soft water, so if you can install a barrel and collect rainwater, do so. There are handy little devices that allow you to connect a barrel to a rain pipe and have an overflow function. The same rule applies to watering containers as to watering a garden: the best time to do it is early in the morning or in the evening. If you water in the middle of the day, the water will evaporate quickly.

Too much water is just as damaging for your plants as too little of it, which is why every container should have drainage holes in the bottom to allow surplus water to flow away. It is also a good idea to put some terracotta pot shards or large pebbles at the bottom of all pots and containers. If surplus water has nowhere to go and the plants sit in wet soil for a longer period of time, their roots might start to rot. When it comes to large containers on a terrace that are also exposed to rain, it is best to raise them slightly by placing them on a couple of bricks or special pot feet to make sure water can drain freely. On the other hand, if your pots are under a roof and only get water when you give it to them, the best solution is to place them in a shallow saucer. You can then water them from underneath and let the water be drawn up by capillary action. This way the leaves of the plants will not get wet (which could lead to fungal disease). If you go away for a day, you can fill up the saucer to the brim and leave a little reserve for your plants. But this does not mean the saucer should continuously be full of water! Let the plants soak up the water and wait a little before you fill up again. You can also buy (or make) a self-watering container, with a little reservoir for water at the bottom of the pot. In a self-watering pot no water is lost to evaporation and you can water less frequently.

Because the amount of fertiliser in potting soil is limited, at some point you have to start giving your plants a little extra. The amount of fertiliser in commercial potting mixes is usually sufficient for about two to three months. If you make your own potting mix that includes (worm) compost, it will probably suffice longer because the nutrients are released more slowly. But do not wait until the leaves of your plants turn yellow and hang sadly to start feeding them! If you process your green waste in a wormery or a bokashi, you are simultaneously making your own liquid fertiliser. The surplus liquid from both a wormery and a bokashi is full of nutrients and can simply be diluted with water to feed your plants. These are the only kinds of liquid fertiliser I've ever used for my containers and the results are excellent. To feed fruiting bushes or trees that remain in the same container for a number of years, I remove the top layer in spring and add a new layer of worm compost every year.

Another liquid fertiliser produced in abundance in every household is urine. If the idea does not freak you out, dilute it with water at a 1:10 ratio and use it to feed your pots. Of course, you should not pour it over the leaves of your lettuce but water from underneath instead so that it is absorbed through the roots. Used this way, freshly produced urine from healthy individuals is safe to use.

Small-scale composting

Compared to a gardener with access to soil, an apartment dweller is rather limited when it comes to recycling nutrients within the household. If you want to turn kitchen waste into feed for your little garden, there are two main ways to go about it: you can either ferment the waste in a bokashi bucket or set up a wormery.

The bokashi bucket is a hermetically-sealed container that means you can keep it in the middle of your kitchen without having to deal with foul odours or other potential unpleasant side-effects of composting. Every time you add kitchen waste to the bucket, you sprinkle a handful of bokashi bran (bran impregnated with effective microorganisms) on top. Herein lies one of the disadvantages of bokashi: though not impossible, it is difficult to make the impregnated bran yourself and that means you have to keep buying it. On the other hand, you do not need large quantities of it and in our household, the two-kilo bags we buy go a long way. One important advantage is that the bokashi can easily handle food waste that might be problematic in a traditional compost heap such as cooked food and even meat. When the bucket is full, we leave it for about two weeks, so that the content can fully ferment. In the meantime, we start filling another bucket. During the fermentation process we tap the surplus liquid through the little tap at the bottom. The liquid has a quite pleasant sweet-sour smell, reminiscent of sauerkraut, which too is a fermented product. It can be used for a variety of things, for example, poured undiluted into the sink it acts as a pipe cleaner. But for a container gardener, the best way to use it is probably as liquid plant feed, diluted with water at a 1:100 ratio.

The fermented content of the bokashi does not look very different from the food waste you put in it but its chemical composition has changed significantly. If you want to use it in the garden, you need to dig a trench, pour the content into it and then cover it with a layer of soil. Within a short period of time, it will decompose completely. If you do not want to dig trenches in your garden, you can add the fermented waste to your compost heap. This is something we often do and it is a great way to speed up the composting process. Within a week, the compost shrinks visibly and in addition to that it is enriched with beneficial microorganisms. Either of these ways of using the fermented food waste are not practical for a balcony grower but luckily, it can also be used to feed plants in large pots and containers. In order to do that, first add a layer of potting mix to your chosen container, then a layer of the fermented food waste and top that with a second layer of potting mix. If your container is very deep (over 30 centimetres), you can repeat the layers several times, but you need to finish with a layer of potting mix. Cover the filled container with something like a piece of tarp to prevent it from getting too wet in the rain and leave it undisturbed for two weeks. After that, you can start sowing or planting. In my experience the bokashi provides nutrients for container grown plants over a long period of time which means it usually takes months before I need to start using liquid feed.

In a wormery, worms are employed to turn your kitchen and garden waste into excellent, nutrient-rich compost. However, these are not the worms you will find in healthy garden soil. The best worms for the job are the so-called redworms or tiger worms (*Eisenia fetida*), often found in decomposing manure. They are slender and reddish and have the biggest appetite among worm species, which means they will do the job the fastest. If they are happy, they will procreate rapidly and a mere handful is enough to start a wormery. Over the years, I have supplied many friends with worms so that they could start their own small-scale composting operation. If you cannot find anybody with a thriving worm population willing to part with a handful, you can also buy worms online and have them shipped to you.

Our wormery is a fairly luxurious model that we got second hand, consisting of four trays stacked on top of each other. The bottom tray serves to catch surplus liquid and the other

three are filled with green waste in various stages of decomposition. When one tray is filled, we put another one on top and start adding vegetable and fruit waste to it. The top three trays all have small holes in the bottom so that the worms can move freely between them. As soon as they process all the waste in a tray, they will move upwards to start on the fresh supply. We can then empty the finished compost and stack the empty tray on top. If you do not want to buy a wormery, you can also quite easily fashion one out of stackable plastic boxes. The worms shy away from light, so dark plastic is preferable. Though the system I described works really well, it is not necessary for a wormery to be multi-storey; even an old dustbin can be converted for this use, just make sure surplus liquid can drain away.

If you do not want your worms to move away in search of greener pastures, you need to create a pleasant work environment. They don't enjoy extreme temperatures, neither too cold, nor too hot, and they do not like it too wet either. You should, of course, also ensure a steady supply of food. Tiger worms will eat most vegetable and fruit scraps and they love coffee grounds. They are not too keen on food that tastes very sharp and sour, so it's often recommended to avoid adding citrus peel. However, I find that if I do not add too much of it at once, citrus peel too will be processed. Interestingly, avocado peel will not. The worms thrive at temperatures around 15°C (60°F) and too cold (sub-zero) or too hot (above 30°C/86°F) can be deadly. If you can, it is therefore best to put your wormery in a garage, shed or cellar during winter, but this is likely not a possibility if you live in an apartment. If you keep your wormery on a balcony, put it in a sheltered corner when it's cold and in a shady spot when it's warm. If necessary, you can also wrap your wormery in bubble wrap to protect it from extreme cold. That being said, our wormery is outside year round, albeit in a sheltered spot against a fence, and I find enough worms will survive even if it freezes. However, cold temperatures mean the worms are less active and the processing of green waste slows down considerably, which is why I add much less material during the winter months. As soon as it gets warmer the pace will pick up again and more can be added. To prevent the wormery from getting too wet, I add some cardboard from time to time, such as egg containers ripped into pieces. The finished worm compost is dark and crumbly and a wonderful addition to the potting mix in your container garden. The surplus liquid that we catch in the bottom tray is full of nutrients too, and an excellent liquid feed, if diluted at a ratio of at least 1:10 with water.

Mulching in containers

In order to prevent the potting soil in your containers from drying out too quickly and to stop weeds from shooting up among your plants, it is a good idea to top your containers with a layer of mulch. I like to use cocoa shells for this purpose because they not only fulfil both purposes mentioned above but also look neat and will supply a bit of extra nutrients every time you water your plants. Another possibility is to use purely decorative materials such as colourful pebbles, marbles or little shells; these will not supply any nutrients but will prevent evaporation and weed growth. Or use organic materials that you can forage for such as pine cones, pine needles or walnut and hazelnut shells: pretty, useful and free.

The right size

Generally speaking, the bigger the container, the more possibilities you have. My advice would therefore be to (whenever possible) use larger containers and grow more plants together, instead of planting them individually in lots of small containers. The bigger the volume of potting soil, the less prone it is to drying out. It is therefore much easier to care for five lettuce plants growing together in a largish container than for five small pots with one lettuce plant each. Even better, try combining different vegetables into mutually beneficial polycultures!

The table below presumes that the width of the containers you use is approximately the same as their depth. But for most plants, the total volume of potting soil is more important than the depth in itself. This means you could grow a courgette plant in a container shallower than the specified 30cm (12in), provided it is wide enough to hold a sufficient amount of soil. However, the same does not apply to root vegetables such as carrots or parsnips, whose roots grow straight down. But if you want to grow carrots and you only have shallow pots, you can opt for the funny round varieties such as 'Paris Market' or the blunt shaped 'Nantes'. For other vegetables too, there are often compact varieties available that were specifically developed for container gardening. While the average bush tomato needs a pot that is 20-25cm (8-10in) deep, the 'Tiny Tim' tomato will happily grow in a pot that is just 15cm (6in) deep.

CONTAINER DEPTH

10cm/4in	Cut-and-come again lettuce, radishes, spring onions, leaf mustard, rocket, corn salad, winter purslane
15cm/6in	Garlic, peas, bush beans, Paris Market carrots, annual herbs such as dill, coriander, basil, parsley and chervil
20cm/8in	Aubergines, endive, turnips, cucumber, leeks, chard, peppers and chillies, broad beans, (bush) tomatoes, Nantes carrots, perennial herbs such as mint, lemon balm and chives
25cm/10in	Beets, broccoli, cauliflower, parsnip, carrot, alpine strawberries
30cm/12in	Courgette, sweet corn, rhubarb, raspberry, cabbages
40cm/16in	Red, white and black currants, grapes, blueberries
50cm/20in	Fig, fruit trees on a dwarfing rootstock: apple, pear, plum, peach

Pots on a balcony and roof terrace

A massive container full of potting soil that gets even heavier when wet, can easily weigh more than a balcony or a roof terrace was designed to handle. If you can, it is therefore best to place heavy pots close to a load-bearing wall, not at the edge of a traversing balcony. When you have doubts about the load-bearing capacity of your balcony, choose lighter containers and a lightweight potting mix. To lessen the weight of potting mix, you can mix in lava grit (up to a third of the total volume). But beware: lighter containers are also less stable and prone to being blown over by strong winds so be sure to anchor or fasten them properly. Wind will also dry out the plants more quickly so you have to monitor them closely and water as needed.

A SOUTH-FACING BALCONY

A balcony facing south gets direct sunlight for most of the day. Especially if it is sheltered from wind, it will be very warm too.

Suited for: all sun-loving herbs (rosemary, oregano, lavender, savory, basil, vervaine) and most vegetables but especially those that need a lot of sun (tomatoes, peppers, sweet corn, aubergine and beans). If there's enough space for a large container, try growing a fig, apricot or a peach.

AN EAST- OR WEST-FACING BALCONY

A balcony facing east receives sun in the morning, a west-facing balcony receives sun in the afternoon. The circumstances are less extreme with neither too much sun nor shade.

Suited for: most vegetables, herbs and fruit, with the exception of those that require a lot of sunlight such as aubergines, peppers or figs.

A NORTH-FACING BALCONY

A balcony facing north receives relatively little direct sunlight and remains fairly cool.

Suited for: some herbs (parsley, lovage, mint, lemon balm, chervil), leafy vegetables (spinach, lettuce, chard, rocket, and kale), peas and broad beans, perennial vegetables that tolerate shade (Good King Henry, sorrel, hosta, rhubarb) and some fruit (summer raspberries, gooseberries, red currant and sour cherry).

CHAPTER 2

Tailor-made Container Gardens

Minimalist herb garden

When aspiring gardeners ask me what to grow when you have little space and zero experience, my answer is always: start with perennial herbs. Those are some of the easiest plants to grow and you can just keep harvesting from the same plants for months. From a financial point of view too, perennial herbs are a great investment. The small bags of herbs you can buy at the supermarket are comparatively expensive not to mention the copious amounts of plastic involved when you buy herbs regularly. Herbs are incredibly versatile in their use and there are few dishes that will not benefit from the addition of some. Moreover, all herbs have medicinal properties that you can employ to support your body's ability to heal and fight all kinds of ailments. While herbs can be surprisingly effective as medicine, they have few side-effects and are usually safe to use even for children. Anybody who complains about a sore throat anywhere near me will be served sage tea and given a bunch of this beneficial herb. The effeciveness of this simple remedy has convinced many a friend in the past of the potency of herbs.

You can grow herbs in individual pots but you can also plant them together in a larger container. Planting up a strawberry pot with herbs saves even more space. You can place the pot on a sunny (south-facing) balcony or in a sunny spot on your terrace – it should get at least six hours of direct sunlight in summer. Proximity to the kitchen is another thing to consider for the sake of convenience. While most strawberry pots available are terracotta, I sought out a glazed one. Not only does its light blue colour contrast prettily with the different herbs, the glaze also means it dries out less quickly.

Because all the plants in the pot have to share the same potting mix and receive the same care, it's important to combine herbs that share the same growing requirements and will thrive under the same circumstances. I limited my selection to Mediterranean herbs such as rosemary, thyme and sage, which all require well-draining, alkaline soil, lots of sun and little fertiliser. To improve drainage, I added some sharp sand to my potting soil and to make it more alkaline, I added about a tablespoon of lime. All the plants I chose are perennial, although some are not completely hardy. During periods of severe frost, I put the pot in a sheltered spot. Other than that, it requires little care.

PLANTING UP THE POT

Most of these herbs can be grown from seed but considering you only need one or two of each kind, it is probably best to buy plants in this case. If you get your plants from a reputable nursery, there should be just one plant with well-developed roots in each pot. However, if you get them from a supermarket for example, there will usually be many plants in each pot, their roots all tangled up and competing for nutrients. In this case, remove them from the pot and gently untangle the roots before planting them individually in your strawberry pot. You will likely have more plants than you need, so you can either pot them up and give them away or immediately use the surplus for cooking.

Cover the drainage hole in the bottom of the pot with terracotta pot shards or some pebbles to prevent it from getting clogged. Then add a layer of your potting soil up to just under the first openings. Put one plant in each opening; the easiest way to do this is usually by pushing/pulling them through the opening from the inside out. Add the next layer of potting soil to cover the roots and continue this way until you have filled all the openings. Save the rosemary plant for the top, since this will be the largest one. Water well and place the pot in a suitable spot. If you put it on a balcony or against a wall, remember to turn it regularly so that all the plants get sufficient sunlight.

THE HERBS

Most herbs are so versatile that even if you grow just a handful, you will be able to season many different dishes and treat various ailments. As experienced herbalists like to say: 'it is better to know ten uses of one herb, than one use of ten different herbs'. When it comes to using herbs in the kitchen, I do not believe in right and wrong combinations. Even though I will suggest some specific uses below, I'd encourage you to experiment and find your own favourite ways to use herbs in your cooking.

Sage (*Salvia officinalis*)

The pointed greyish leaves and purple flowers of common sage are in themselves quite decorative but if you don't think that's enough, there is also golden, variegated or even tri-colour sage. Sadly, whenever breeders concern themselves with the appearance of a plant, other properties such as taste and healing powers may suffer.

In the kitchen, sage goes well with fish, pork or minced meat, or for the vegetarians among us, it tastes great with potatoes and winter squash too. Medicinally, sage is strongly antibacterial and antiseptic. An infusion drunk as tea or used for gargling helps if you have a sore throat or laryngitis. It is also effective against diarrhoea and furthermore, it helps against excessive sweating, which makes it a good herb for regular use during menopause.

Oregano (*Origanum vulgare*)

Even though marjoram (*Origanum majorana*) is more aromatic than wild oregano, it is also considerably less hardy and therefore less suited for this perennial planting. Of the different cultivars of oregano available, 'Compactum' is my favourite because it comes closest in taste to marjoram. Oregano has small rounded leaves and pale pink flowers that are a favourite with bees. It is popular in all Mediterranean cuisines, often used in Italian tomato sauces, on pizza, or in the Greek favourite, moussaka. Medicinally, its antispasmodic properties make it effective against stomach and bowel ailments and adding it to a heavy dish will aid digestion. It is also a calming herb that can be used to relieve nervousness and insomnia.

Thyme (*Thymus*)

Both the narrow-leaved common thyme (*Thymus vulgaris*) and lemon thyme (*Thymus citriodorus*) have a delicious scent, the lemon variety with the added notes of citrus. Together with bay leaf and parsley, thyme forms the base of bouquet garni, a small bunch of herbs used in French cuisine to flavour soups and stews. But frankly, you could add thyme to just about any dish, including a fruit compote, and the dish would likely benefit from it. As a medicinal herb, thyme is just as versatile: it is a powerful disinfectant and a great tonic for the whole body when used regularly. A strong brew added to bath water will help against all kinds of skin problems, and used internally it will fight off infection. I most often use thyme to treat colds and coughs, prepared either as tea (maybe with a little honey) or as syrup.

Winter savory (*Satureja montana*)

This hardy variety of savory is a little coarser but just as aromatic as its annual counterpart, summer savory (*Satureja hortensis*), and much more reliable as a garden plant. I like to add a few sprigs of savory whenever I'm cooking beans – not only for the slightly peppery aroma but also because savory aids digestion and helps to prevent flatulence, the

Oregano

unpleasant side-effect of eating the good-for-you pulses. For the same reason, savory is a good accompaniment to greasy dishes that are difficult to digest. Another way to use this herb is to rub it into your skin to soothe insect bites.

Rosemary (*Rosmarinus officinalis*)

The needles of rosemary are highly aromatic and in the kitchen, a little goes a long way. Because the herb is evergreen, I tend to use it a lot during the colder months when other herbs can't be harvested fresh. But beware, rosemary is not fully hardy and needs a sheltered spot and good drainage to survive severe frosts. For growing in pots, try to seek out one of the more compact varieties.

Some of my favourite ways to use rosemary in the kitchen are adding a few sprigs to potatoes or vegetables roasting in the oven, or stirring some finely chopped rosemary into tomato soup or risottos. I also love rosemary cake with a heaped tablespoon of finely chopped rosemary

Winter savory

Hyssop

added to the batter – this may sound a little weird but it works! Because of its many uses, rosemary is also a favourite with herbalists. It stimulates the brain and aids memory, it is a tonic for the heart and helps against high blood pressure. We often make rosemary tea with a sprig of lavender when one of us has a headache (it is also effective in case of a hangover).
A strong brew added to the bath will stimulate blood circulation and rosemary-infused oil can be used to massage painful muscles.

Lavender (*Lavandula angustifolia*)

There are countless varieties of lavender, such as the funny looking *Lavandula stoechas* with a tuft of flowers on top or *Lavandula dentata* with 'toothed' leaves but these are often not fully hardy. The 'real' lavender (*Lavandula angustifolia*) is the best choice for our little garden because of its hardiness, heady scent and medicinal properties.

In the kitchen, lavender is often used in desserts: to flavour shortbread, ice cream and cake. But in Provence it is also added to savoury dishes, such as roasted lamb. Medicinally, lavender is mostly known for its calming properties and tea (or a bath) made with lavender relieves stress, headache and nervousness. I often add lavender to my bath after a stressful day to prevent insomnia. But the herb is also a powerful disinfectant and a brew can be used to wash wounds to prevent infection.

Hyssop (*Hyssopus officinalis*)

Hyssop is, in my opinion, an unjustly overlooked herb that isn't grown enough. The narrow leaves and intensely blue flowers (there is also a white and a pink variety) taste slightly bitter but are very aromatic. I like to add a little to tomato sauce for pizza and other Italian dishes. The herb is particularly effective against deep-seated cough but also many other ailments of the respiratory system. Crushed leaves can be applied to bruises and insect bites.

Regularly adding herbs to the food we eat is a great way to, in the words of the Greek physician Hippocrates, 'turn our food into our medicine'. This will hopefully help to prevent disease, but herbs can also be applied curatively when you catch a cold, have a headache or have an upset stomach. Here are some simple ways to prepare herbal remedies for which you do not need any special equipment or ingredients.

Herbal remedies

Herbal tea

In our household, herbal tea is the drink of choice. In summer, we go into the garden every morning to pick a few sprigs for tea, and in winter we use dried herbs stored in glass jars. Most of the time, which herb we use is dictated by taste, but when somebody complains of a headache, we will prepare rosemary and lavender. Thyme and hyssop will be prescribed for a cough, sage for a sore throat and oregano and savory for an upset stomach. Making herbal tea is no exact science since you can never even know what the exact content of the different substances is at any given moment. The instructions below are therefore only approximate. It is obviously also easier to prepare a larger amount of tea at once.

For 1 cup

5 leaves or about a 5cm-long sprig of fresh herbs
1 cup (250ml) water

Bring water to boil and pour it over the herbs. Cover to prevent the aromatic oils from escaping and let steep. About 10-15 minutes is enough if you're just making tea to drink, but if you want to use it medicinally, allow it to steep longer, 30-60 minutes.

Herbal syrup

The first herbal remedy I ever made when I started experimenting with the medicinal properties of herbs as a teenager was thyme syrup. Unlike some other medicines, this is a delicious tasting remedy that both children and adults will gladly take. The recipe works for other herbs too, for example oregano or mint.

Make an infusion according to the instructions above but use double the amount of herbs and let them steep longer. Strain the liquid and add 1 cup of honey (or sugar) to every cup of the infusion. Heat gently to mix well. For a longer shelf life, you can also add a little brandy. Pour the syrup into a clean glass bottle (or a jar) and store in the refrigerator. It will last for several weeks, even months.

Herbal oil

Finely chop your herbs and place them in a glass jar. Cover the herbs completely with oil (olive oil is best for this). Close the jar and put it in a warm, sunny spot. Let the herbs steep for two weeks. Strain the oil and pour it into a clean jar. If you want an even stronger oil, repeat the process by pouring the strained oil over a fresh batch of herbs. Store the oil in a cool and dark place.

Basil – the royal herb

Compared to all the aforementioned Mediterranean herbs, this beloved half-hardy annual needs a lot more moisture, nutrients and heat. This means it is better to grow basil either in a pot on its own, or mixed with sun-loving vegetables such as in one of the following polycultures. If you buy plants, you'll usually get the Genovese type of basil, which is excellent for Italian dishes and for pesto in particular. But if you start your plants from seed, there are many more varieties to choose from: 'Mrs Burn's Lemon' and 'Lemonade' have a strong citrus flavour and make delicious tea. Thai basil has hints of aniseed and cloves in its flavour spectrum and is a great flavouring for curry dishes. Cinnamon basil goes well with sweet dishes and the large leaves of 'Mammoth' basil can be added to salads or sandwiches. Apart from those annual varieties, there are also perennial basils such as 'African Blue' and 'Magic Mountain'. They are not hardy but can be successfully overwintered on a sunny windowsill.

A GARDEN IN A TUB

Many years ago we bought a large zinc tub at a flea market. When my kids were young, I would put it in the garden, fill it with water and let them splash to their hearts' delight. But when they outgrew this kind of entertainment, I started using the tub for growing edibles. Every year I delight in coming up with a different planting and creating a new miniature garden: one year I grew a succession of salads, another year a colourful mix of edible flowers. Instead of growing just one kind of vegetable or herb, I often plant polycultures that will provide a varied harvest. Because the tub is literally just three metres away from our back door, I pass it multiple times every day and the plants always get the attention they need. The closeness to the kitchen also means that it is very easy to pop out while making dinner and pick some leaves for a salad or edible flowers for garnish. It is impossible to beat the freshness of produce that is grown so close to where it's eaten!

Before filling the tub, I drilled several holes in the bottom. Next, I put in a layer of gravel and covered that with a piece of woven landscape fabric (this prevents the gravel and potting mix from mixing and makes it easier to reuse the soil). I also set the tub on a couple of bricks so that it can drain freely. The tub is 70cm (27.5in) long, 55cm (21.5in) wide and 30cm (12in) high, and requires a fair amount of potting mix. I start with a commercial potting mix but add lots of our homemade worm compost and some sharp sand too. These additions improve both the water holding capacity and the drainage of the mix. I reuse the potting mix several years in a row, always adding about 25-30% of fresh worm compost. After planting up the container, I add a layer of mulch (usually cocoa shells) to slow down evaporation so that the container does not need to be watered quite as often. During the growing season I apply liquid fertiliser, either diluted waste liquid from our wormery (1:10) or from the bokashi (1:100).

Year round salad bar

When it comes to salads, the difference between homegrown 'fresh' and store-bought 'fresh' is even more staggering than in other vegetables. Wilted leaves with brown edges in plastic bags that have been lying on the shelf in the store for days in no way resemble the vibrant, freshly harvested stuff. Less obvious but no less important is the difference in vitamin content. Vitamin C especially is very unstable and degrades quickly from the moment plants have been harvested. Consequently, the fresher your salad, the more nutrients it will contain and the better for you it will be.

If you choose an appropriate salad plant for every season and apply different harvesting methods, you can be harvesting fresh salad leaves for most of the year. In this planting, it means sowing and harvesting different varieties of mustard greens as cut-and-come-again in spring, then planting lettuce and picking individual lettuce leaves in summer. For a winter harvest you can sow corn salad and winter purslane, some of the hardiest greens around. My tub is relatively large and allows for variation but you could also simplify the planting for a smaller container by, for example, sowing just one variety of mustard and planting just a few lettuces. Ideally, the container should be in a sunny spot in spring, autumn and winter, but in a partly shaded one during the summer months.

SPRING: MUSTARD GREENS

As soon as the weather warms up a bit, I start sowing mustard greens in wide parallel drills about 10cm (4in) apart. For my most recent planting I chose a colourful mix of six different varieties: 'Pink Lettucy', 'Ruby Streaks', 'Golden Streaks', 'Osaka Purple' and purple mizuna as well as the well-known rocket. Another possibility is to buy a packet of mixed mustard greens and broadcast the seeds. In this case some thinning will likely be necessary but that is no problem as the tiny seedlings make for nice eating too. Mustard greens are some of the fastest growing vegetables and you can often start harvesting them as early as four weeks after sowing. Do this by cutting the leaves approximately two centimetres above the ground, then let the plants regrow. Depending on the variety and weather conditions, you can expect about three cuts before the plants start to bolt.

SUMMER: LETTUCE

Around mid-June, when the mustards start running to seed, I pull them out and plant lettuce that has been pre-sown on the windowsill in April. Of course, you can also buy plants if you lack space for starting seed but your choice of varieties will be more limited. The best types of lettuce to grow here are those suitable for leaf-by-leaf harvesting. To ensure variety in colour and texture, I chose a mix of loose-leaf, iceberg and romaine lettuces ('Pinokkio', 'Claremont', 'Flame' and 'Jack Ice'), fitting a total of 23 plants into my container. By repeatedly picking just the outer leaves from each plant instead of harvesting whole heads, I could keep harvesting from the same plants for many weeks. This is also why the plants can grow so close together: the continual harvesting means they'll never get too big.

AUTUMN/WINTER: CORN SALAD AND WINTER PURSLANE

Around the end of August is a good time to start the last salads of the season: winter purslane (also known as claytonia or miner's lettuce) and corn salad (also called lamb's lettuce or mâche). There are two methods to do this: either you can sow both corn salad and winter purslane directly into the container in rows spaced about 10-15cm (4-6in) apart, or you can start the plants in modules or a seed tray and transplant them later, spacing the individual plants 10cm (4in) apart in both directions. If you sow directly, you can start to harvest by thinning some plants and letting others grow bigger. If you plant individual plants, you can cut the leaves repeatedly, letting the plants regrow. In a sheltered spot (for example against a south-facing wall) the plants will regrow faster and provide more pickings.

Edible flowers

The most colourful my tub has ever been was during the summer I filled it with edible flowers. I want my garden to be both productive and beautiful and nowhere else are these two attributes better united than in the form of flowers that you can eat too. Edible flowers are fragile things that do not keep or ship well, which means you'll hardly ever find them in a store and if you do, the price will likely be exorbitant. Growing them yourself means you can use the flowers lavishly on a daily basis, whereas if you had to buy them, this would be an eccentric luxury. Luckily, most of the best known and most useful edible flowers are actually very easy to grow. You can either sow the flowers directly into the container in which you want to grow them, or pre-sow them in modules on a windowsill. I prefer to do the latter, starting my plants in March/April and transplanting them outside in April/May. You can either grow each kind in a separate pot, or as I did, mix them into a colourful medley. In my tub I planted eight different kinds of edible flowers, just two or three plants of each. As soon as they start to flower, it's time to harvest. Harvesting the flowers equals 'deadheading' in terms of ornamental planting, so if you keep picking, your plants will keep flowering. Given the chance, most of these will also later self-sow.

MY FAVOURITE EDIBLE FLOWERS

Technically, any flower that is not poisonous is edible but not every edible flower is good to eat. Here are my favourites among the annual flowers plus some suggestions on how to use them.

Pot marigold (*Calendula officinalis*)

Pot marigold is the embodiment of joy – just looking at its bright colour improves my mood! Though originally pot marigolds came only in orange-yellow, there are many cultivars available now, ranging in colour from cream to apricot to red(dish). If you want to use marigold medicinally, stick with the wild form but otherwise the double cultivars in mixes such as 'Pink Surprise' or 'Touch of Red' will give you a lot more petals per flower. From the single flowered cultivars, 'Indian Prince' with a contrasting dark centre is a beautiful cut flower and a firm favourite of mine.

The taste of calendula is less remarkable than its appearance and even slightly bitter. To use it in the kitchen, just pull the petals away from the flower centre and scatter them over salads, mix them into butter or cream cheese, add them to rice as 'poor-man's saffron' or stir them into batter for cakes and muffins.

Heartsease (*Viola tricolor*)

The tiny flowers in a combination of yellow, purple and white are produced abundantly, as long as you keep picking. The plants are quite hardy and can be sown both in early spring (March-April) or in autumn for overwintering. The autumn sown plants will give you an extra early harvest. Heartsease will keep on flowering longer if the soil is moist and cool.

The flowers have a fairly neutral taste and go with almost anything. You can of course add them to salads but they also make charming decoration for cakes, tarts and other desserts. For this they can be crystallised in sugar to last longer.

Borage *(Borago officinalis)*

An easy to grow annual that will reliably reappear in the garden. The leaves have the same pleasant cucumber-like flavour as the flowers but are unpleasantly hairy.

You can either carefully pull the pretty star-shaped flowers from the calyx or, if you don't mind the tiny hairs on the stem, cut them just under the flower. Unsurprisingly, borage pairs well with cucumber and I like to add the flowers to cucumber soup or simple cucumber appetisers. They will also make a pretty garnish for fruit salads.

Sweet William *(Dianthus barbatus)*

This staple of the cottage garden is a biennial, meaning it starts flowering in its second year. If left in the ground though, the plant will often flower again in its third year too. There are varieties in all shades of pink, white and red, single or double. To be able to pick the flowers from May/June onwards, you need to sow the seeds a whole year prior to that, or buy plants in spring that will flower in the same year.

Sweet William's petals have a faint clove aroma and are a good addition to both savoury and sweet dishes. They can be used in salads, cakes, syrups, puddings and flower butters.

Nasturtium (*Tropaeolum majus*)

Now, here's a plant that earns its keep! All the parts are edible: leaves, seed pods and flowers and it is powerfully medicinal too. There are climbing varieties (useful when you want to cover an ugly fence) but also compact varieties great for growing in pots. I like the cultivars with variegated leaves such as 'Alaska' and use both the leaves and flowers in salads. The whole plant has a peppery taste. Try filling the flowers with cream cheese or chop them up and stir into potato mash.

Annual clary (*Salvia viridis*)

The colourful parts that we pick in this case are actually not the flowers themselves (which are tiny), but the flower bracts. There are pink, purple and white varieties to choose from. Clary sage germinates easily and can be sown directly from April. It will also self-sow and because it is quite hardy, young seedlings will often survive the winter and flower extra early the next spring. The taste of clary is quite aromatic and slightly bitter. It is best used sparingly in mixed salads.

Rocket (*Eruca sativa*)

This well-known salad plant germinates and grows quickly and bolts even quicker as soon as the weather warms up. The leaves tend to become too hot to be enjoyable but there is no need to pull it out immediately – enjoy the flowers instead. Those too have a cress-like flavour, though less pronounced than the leaves. Rocket is best suited to savoury dishes: you can, for example, use the flowers as a garnish for (pasta) salads, in omelettes or in tomato soup.

Shungiku or Japanese chrysanthemum (*Chrysanthemum japonicum*)

In Japan this annual is usually grown for its leaves but the flowers too are edible. The plant tolerates low temperatures and can be sown early in the growing season. Japanese chrysanthemum also makes a pretty and long-lasting cut flower.

The small pale yellow flowers are somewhat bitter and have an unusual aroma that, to be frank, not everybody enjoys. Try adding them to salads, soups or stir fries.

EDIBLE FLOWERS IN THE KITCHEN

Edible flowers are best picked shortly before you want to use them – a good reason to grow them in close proximity to the kitchen! If however, you do not want to use them straight away, you can leave short stems when cutting and put them in a small vase in a cool spot, or store them in the refrigerator, sandwiched between layers of moist paper towels. Some flowers (for example calendula) can also be dried. Another possibility is to freeze flowers in ice cubes and serve them with ice tea. Instead of in water, you can also freeze them in an ice tray filled with olive oil and use them to garnish soups.

Flowery salad

A variety of lettuce leaves in different shapes and colours (romaine, oakleaf), small leaves left whole, large ones torn in pieces
Several nasturtium leaves (variegated are the prettiest) and other greens such as rocket or mustard
Edible flowers: nasturtium, rocket, calendula (just the petals), heartsease, borage, clary

DRESSING

2 tbsp white wine vinegar
5 tbsp mild olive oil
Pinch of salt and freshly ground black pepper

Whisk together the ingredients for the dressing, check seasoning, and adjust to your preference. In a large bowl, toss the lettuce and any other greens you're using gently with the dressing. Scatter the edible flowers on top.

Edible flower canapés

I like to make these for a Midsummer celebration – they are always a hit. You can prepare the cream cheese mixture in advance, but don't make the canapés too long before serving. The toast tends to go soft, so if you do need to make them ahead of time, sandwich bread would be a better option.

180g/6oz cream cheese
Salt
2 tbsp fresh chives, finely chopped
1 packet melba toast or a few slices of sandwich bread, crusts removed and cut into small rectangles/triangles
Edible flowers such as: borage, nasturtium, calendula (just the petals), rocket, heartsease
Herb leaves: dill, fennel, chervil, nasturtium leaves

In a medium bowl, beat the cream cheese with a wooden spoon. If it's very thick, add a tablespoon of milk to achieve an easily spreadable consistency. Add the chives and salt to taste. Spread the cream cheese mixture on the toast (or bread) and decorate with edible flowers and herb leaves. Keep in the refrigerator until needed (but not too long!).

Cucumber & borage canapés

Even easier than the canapés above and also very low in calories.

400g/14oz cottage cheese
Salt
1 cucumber
A small handful of borage flowers

Season the cottage cheese with salt to taste. Cut the cucumber in about 1cm thick slices. Put about ½ tablespoon of cottage cheese on each slice and decorate with a borage flower. I like to serve the canapés on variegated nasturtium leaves.

thriller

filler

spiller

Polycultures

The two following examples show an even more varied planting: they are polycultures mixing vegetables with herbs and edible flowers. A mixed planting like this provides a nicely varied harvest and makes a better use of the available space but my main reason for creating polycultures is that it generally means fewer disease and pest problems than when growing just one kind of plant.

Because I want my containers not only to produce lots of food but also to be visually attractive, I approach the planting in the same way one would approach an ornamental planting. I like to combine edible plants that provide a variety of leaf shapes, colours and growth habit. Usually, I will include plants with an upright growth habit (structure), some clump-forming plants (volume) and trailing plants (to tumble over the edge of the container). You can also think of these types of plants as a 'thriller', a 'filler' and a 'spiller'.

Variation on the three sisters

The first planting was inspired by the well-known polyculture called 'the three sisters' wherein Native Americans combined their three main food plants (corn, beans and squash) into a mutually beneficial whole. The beans were sown close to the corn so that they could use the corn stalk as support, while the nitrogen-fixing beans supplied extra nutrients for the hungry crop. The trailing squash covered the ground and prevented weed growth and evaporation. Because my tub is too small for a squash plant, I opted for a bush tomato instead and added basil and nasturtium for more variety. Since the plants in this polyculture are not hardy, they are best pre-sown on a sunny windowsill and planted out when frost no longer threatens. In our climate that means planting around mid-May.

4 x SWEETCORN

I usually sow corn towards the end of April or at the beginning of May to plant out two to three weeks later. I put two seeds in each pot and if both germinate, I pull one out. For a container this size, you only need three or four plants and they are best planted in a triangle or a square for good pollination. There are many different kinds of corn: for fresh eating, for popcorn or for grinding into flour. Of course, you can plant anything you want, but since the harvest is small, I opted for sweet corn that is so delicious when absolutely fresh. The compact variety 'Golden Midget' is especially well suited to container growing.

4 x BEANS

You can sow any climbing beans next to your corn plants but I like to sow runner beans because they can be harvested in many ways and at different stages. Even the flowers are delicious but of course, if you pick them all, you won't get any beans. Most varieties of beans will grow taller than the corn (especially if you grow a compact variety like 'Golden Midget'), so you'll have to pinch out the tops. Sow the beans when your corn is about 15-20cm (6-8in) tall.

2 x BASIL

Basil is best sown at the end of March or beginning of April and it requires quite warm temperatures to germinate. I use my small bottom-heated propagator for this. The two varieties in my container are the purple 'Dark Opal' and a green 'Aroma' basil, which is the classic Genovese type, but has an improved disease resistance.

2 x NASTURTIUM

Even just two nasturtium plants will give you plenty of edible flowers and peppery leaves to pick. They are less sensitive to cold than the other plants in this polyculture so you could also sow these directly. As always, compact varieties are best for container growing. You can sow the 'Tom Thumb mixed' and let yourself be surprised by the colour of the flowers, or you can carefully select a cultivar to either match or contrast the rest of your planting. Apart from the aforementioned 'Alaska' with variegated foliage, I like the deep red flowers of 'Princess of India' or 'Salmon Baby' with salmon-pink flowers and dark green foliage, but there are many other compact varieties to choose from.

1 x BUSH TOMATO

You only need one tomato plant so it would make sense to buy it, but if you choose to grow it yourself from seed you have more options. I chose the ultra-early bush tomato 'Ida Gold' which produces the first ping-pong-ball sized orange fruits from the first week of July. A bush tomato will not grow too big and there's no need to remove the side shoots. I sow my tomatoes towards the end of March for planting out around mid-May, together with the corn and basil.

Mini potager

In this planting I put special emphasis on contrasting colours. The red stems of the chard next to the green-grey kale, the feathery dill and brightly orange-red marigolds are as beautiful as any ornamental planting. But there are other benefits to this combination than purely aesthetic: for example, the strong scent of 'Red Gem' marigolds confuses pests that might otherwise be attracted by the kale and both the marigold and dill attract beneficial insects as well.

Because all the plants can be harvested continually (I pick the outer leaves of the chard, kale and lettuce instead of harvesting the whole plant), the planting will look pretty over a long period of time. In this case too, I prefer to sow the plants in April in modules and plant them out in May.

3 x KALE 'NERO DI TOSCANA'

The best thing about this Italian heirloom is its colour – the green-grey crinkled leaves contrast beautifully with the red stems of the chard. Luckily, the taste is also pretty good.

3 x RED CHARD

The variety I used is called 'Fantasy' which I like for its mild taste, mildew-tolerance and relatively thin stems, but there are other red varieties that could be substituted (though you might need less than three plants). I love chard because it is such an incredibly easy to grow, productive and versatile vegetable (as well as being one of the prettiest veggies).

3 x LETTUCE 'ELYBURG'

This lettuce is a cross between iceberg and cos and has an upright growing habit and crisp leaves. As mentioned before, I do not harvest the whole heads, but pick the outer leaves instead in order to prolong the harvest. Just about any cos (for example 'Claremont') or loose-leaf lettuce could be substituted here.

2 x DILL (*Anethum graveolens*)

Both the leaves and the seeds of this annual herb are edible; I like to add the finely chopped leaves to grain-based salads and the dill flowers to pickles. As a member of the umbelliferae family, dill also attracts hoverflies whose larvae prey on aphids.

1 x MARIGOLD 'RED GEM' (*Tagetes tenuifolia*)

Marigolds are a great companion plant but I do not like the big-flowered top-heavy varieties. This one however with its cloud of tiny red flowers is pretty and both the leaves and the flowers have a pleasant citrus flavour.

1 x NASTURTIUM

I do not remember the name of this orange-flowered variety but any compact cultivar would be suitable. The growing habit of the plants means they will trail prettily over the edge of the container.

Chard pancakes with goat cheese and nasturtiums

PANCAKE BATTER:

240g/1½ cups buckwheat flour
3 large eggs
500ml/2 cups whole milk
250ml/1 cup water
1 tbsp olive oil
Pinch of salt
A small bunch of chard (about 10 leaves), stalks removed

FILLING:

140g/5oz fresh goat cheese
180ml/¾ cup Greek yogurt
A heaped spoonful of finely chopped dill
A handful of roughly chopped nasturtium flowers

To make the batter, combine all ingredients in a blender and mix on high speed until smooth. Leave to rest in the fridge for half an hour (you can keep it much longer though).

To fry the pancakes, heat a little oil in a skillet and pour in enough batter to cover the pan with a thin layer. Wait until the top sets and the edges begin to turn golden brown, then flip the pancake and cook until the other side is golden brown too. Repeat until you've used all of the batter.

To make the filling, put the goat cheese in a medium bowl and stir to loosen. Add the Greek yogurt and whisk until smooth. Stir in the dill and nasturtiums and season to taste.

Spread a heaped tablespoon of the filling on one half of a pancake, than fold it twice into quarters. Use the remaining flowers to decorate.

Flower bulb lasagne

Even though the petals of tulips are edible, this last planting I want to share is, unlike all the previous ones, primarily ornamental. Edibility notwithstanding, there are good reasons to add spring bulbs to your container garden. Because of their early flowering, many spring bulbs are an important source of nectar for bees, at a time when there is little food around. Equally important for me is the way they rekindle my enthusiasm for gardening. The crocuses flowering in February are an invitation to get outside and start gardening again. Because different bulbs require different planting depths, you can plant them on top of each other as a kind of lasagne. A pot of 25cm deep is sufficient for two layers, but if you want to plant three, your container should be at least 30cm deep. My planting combines crocuses with daffodils and tulips, which means continuous flowering from February/March till May. Other, less common spring bulbs could be used too, such as grape hyacinth (*Muscari*), iris, glory of the snow (*Chionodoxa*), or squill (*Scilla*). Because the bulbs can be planted in late autumn (I usually plant them in November) and finish flowering around the beginning of May, this planting can follow and/or precede another one. You can plant the bulbs after you have harvested your last tomatoes and after the first frost has killed your nasturtiums. And in May, after the tulips finish flowering, there's still plenty of time to plant one of the polycultures or a mix of edible flowers.

HOW TO PLANT

On the right you will find step-by-step instructions on how to plant the bulbs. The amounts are for my tub (70 x 55cm/27.5 x 21.5in and 30cm/12in deep). If your container is smaller, reduce the number of bulbs in proportion. The choice of varieties is based on my personal preferences – I love scented daffodils with double blooms and consider lily-flowered tulips to be especially elegant. But there are many wonderful varieties to choose from and you can cook up a totally different lasagne to suit your own taste. As in the other plantings, I first add a layer of gravel to the tub – drainage is especially important for bulbs that will sit in the container all winter. The bulbs are planted in reverse order to their flowering times – the latest flowering ones make up the bottom layer, the earliest flowerers go on top.

LATER CARE

Check the potting soil during the winter for moisture and water if necessary – in our climate it hardly ever needs watering. In early spring, when the first plants start appearing, move the container into a light spot. Water regularly and, when the bulbs start flowering, you might want to spoil them with a little homemade liquid fertiliser. When the last tulips finish flowering, you can (if you are not going to plant something else straight away) wait until the foliage turns yellow and dies down and only then dig out the bulbs. Let them dry and in autumn you can plant them again outside in the garden (it's better to use fresh bulbs for the lasagne). Because I grow a bulb lasagne like this every year, I've been able to gradually increase the carpet of crocuses along the main path in my backyard.

Tulips

First, spread a layer of potting mix about 5cm (2in) thick at the bottom of your container (on top of the gravel covered with a piece of landscape fabric). Space 20 tulip bulbs evenly over the surface. The bulbs should not be touching and neither should they be too close to the edge of the container, since that might cause them to freeze. I planted 'White Triumphator', a white lily-flowered tulip.

Daffodils

Cover the tulip bulbs with a layer of potting mix and water well if the mix is dry. Add 12 daffodil bulbs, spread evenly over the tub. I chose 'Sir Winston Churchill', a double flowered daffodil with several fragrant creamy-white flowers on each stem.

Crocuses

Spread a layer of potting mix on top of the daffodil bulbs and make it moist. The last bulbs to be planted are 50 crocuses. To extend their flowering, I combined two different cultivars, the mauve and grey 'Vanguard', which is one of the earliest crocuses to flower, and the deep purple 'Flower Record'.

Top layer and mulch

Top the crocus bulbs with a final layer of potting mix, about 5cm (2in) thick. I like to add a layer of mulch too, for example cacao shells or hazelnut shells. To prevent the bulbs from freezing, place your container in a sheltered spot. I put mine against a wall in a corner sheltered from wind behind our house. If severe frost threatens, it pays to cover the container with a reed mat or bubble wrap but remove those as soon as the temperature rises again.

part 2
The Permaculture Kitchen Garden

Once you can get access to garden soil, the possibilities will expand exponentially. It does not necessarily mean you must have a backyard – maybe you can rent an allotment nearby or maybe there's a community garden in your neighbourhood? Or maybe there's someone willing to share their yard?

If you then employ permaculture principles and techniques in designing and running your garden, you'll not only save yourself a ton of work but will also have a positive impact on your surroundings and benefit the environment at large. In the broadest sense, permaculture is a design framework inspired by natural ecosystems. Kitchen gardens where mostly annuals are grown are arguably quite far removed from a natural ecosystem, but even here there are lessons from nature we can adopt. Abstaining from digging and the use of mulch are natural ways to gradually build a healthy, well-structured, 'living' soil wherein your plants can thrive. Amplifying diversity by planting (carefully designed) polycultures instead of monocultures prevents disease and pest damage. Re-purposing old materials and upcycling garden waste to create compost, catching and storing rainwater, making use of microclimates are all simple ways to conserve energy and save money too. Carefully thought out design decisions, which place the individual elements in the best location relative to one another, will create countless beneficial relationships and give maximum return for minimum action.

In the following three chapters, you'll find all the information you need to start a no-dig garden and cultivate vegetables in permanent beds. You'll also learn how to manage time and space well, in order to maximise the harvest from your plot. Which, by the way, does not mean that your garden cannot be beautiful too: maybe you'll want to plant a colourful polyculture or even start a proper potager.

CHAPTER 3

A Good Start

The best place for your garden

In an ideal world, where you'd be free to choose where you start your kitchen garden, you would choose a spot that is gently sloping to the south, for maximum sun exposure. The soil would be loam rich in humus with a pH around 6.5 (slightly acidic). It would hold moisture well but be well-draining at the same time. Your garden would be open to the sun, but protected from the wind. There would be a convenient source of water because who wants to be hauling buckets of water over a long distance? It would also be great if this garden of yours was close to the kitchen because that would make it easy to pick a bunch of herbs when you're making dinner or gather a salad just before you sit down to eat.

The chances are slim that the spot where you're starting your garden fulfils all these requirements. But do not despair – even a less than ideal plot can usually be improved enough to make successful gardening possible. If your garden is too exposed, you can plant a hedge that will serve as a windbreak. Poor soil can be improved by adding lots of organic matter and acidity can be corrected with lime. If drainage is poor, it might be enough to construct raised beds. The only problem that is hard to do something about is lack of sunlight, especially if it is caused by shadows cast by buildings. Most vegetables need a minimum of six hours of direct sunlight per day and if your garden gets less, growing annual vegetables will be tricky. You can concentrate on a handful of greens that can get by with less, such as chard or kale, but not even those will thrive in full shade. Another option is growing shade-tolerant perennial vegetables many of which are less demanding than annuals and will grow reasonably well even under less than ideal conditions.

The size

It's easy to get carried away in spring and set up a garden that will require much more time to care for than you bargained for. The garden then becomes a source of frustration and guilt instead of pleasure and satisfaction. Which is why probably the most important piece of advice for aspiring gardeners is: 'Start small'. Nothing is as discouraging as a kitchen garden with more weeds than vegetables in it, a garden that you simply can't keep up with.

A small, well-tended kitchen garden will very likely be more productive than a garden that is too large for you to care for properly. Even just a single bed of $2m^2$ ($21ft^2$) can produce a surprising amount of food, especially if you grow a polyculture. If your ambition and the space you have available are bigger, you can, for example, start with a plot of $15m^2$ ($160ft^2$) and expand this as you gain more experience. However, if you rent a plot in a community garden, it might be a

Even a small garden can be very productive, especially if you fit in at least two plantings per season

lot larger than this; here in the Netherlands, allotment gardens are typically 100 or even 200m² (1,000 or 2,000ft²). In that case, you might want to use only a part of it for growing during the first season and cover the rest with clearance mulch, which will kill any weeds in the meantime.

The picture will look different if your ambition is to be completely self-sufficient in vegetables: how many square metres do you need then? Obviously, many different factors come into play. Not every soil is equally fertile – it might take a few years to build up really good soil. Not every year is equally favourable – late frosts or summer draught might make a considerable dent in your projected harvest. Climate is important too – mild winters will allow for year round growing and harvesting while colder ones will limit your possibilities.

My father jokes that one square metre would be enough for him to grow all the vegetables he needs, but even though he does not love vegetables as much as I do, he would in reality need far more space to grow what he eats. I am a vegetarian with a plant-based diet and my family consumes a lot of vegetables. As a rule of thumb, you can consider 50m² (540ft²) per person, which works out at 200m² (2,160ft²) for a family of four. In order for this space to produce enough food though, you'll have to set it up efficiently. Growing in raised beds that can be planted intensively is more productive than the traditional row system, which requires space between rows for walking. The production will also be much higher if you fit in at least two plantings per season and keep the soil in optimum condition.

Soil as the basis

Successful gardening starts literally from the bottom up: with the soil. This living, unbelievably intricate thin layer covering our planet on which our lives play out and to which we are connected in numerous ways. Most soils originate from rock, which has over the course of millennia and under the influence of water, frost and wind, been ground into tiny particles. The size of these particles determines the character of the soil: sandy soil consists of comparatively large particles (between 0.5 and 2mm) while the particles in clay are far smaller (less than 0.002mm). The other three main components of soil are air, water and organic matter. But soil is more than a sum of substances: it is a living whole. Just a teaspoon of healthy soil contains more microorganisms than there are people walking the earth. Besides the creatures visible to the naked eye, such as worms and insects, there are countless microscopic organisms such as bacteria, fungi, nematodes and algae.

These tiny organisms help to aerate the soil, decompose organic waste and make nutrients available for plants. The more 'alive' the soil is, the more fertile it will be. And while it is hardly possible for us to understand all the intricate relationships and complex processes going on in the soil (and luckily also not necessary for successful gardening), it is essential to handle soil with care and respect.

We need to create optimum conditions for soil life by making sure our garden soil is neither too dry nor too wet, that the acidity is not extreme and that there is plenty of organic matter available. The use of pesticides, fungicides and synthetic fertilisers must be avoided, as well as unnecessary soil disturbance, since they all damage the invisible but indispensable web of life in the soil, on which our plants, our gardens and in the end we ourselves, depend.

The soil in our garden is sand, which means it drains well but it does not contain a lot of nutrients and it is prone to acidification

Soil types

	ADVANTAGES	DISADVANTAGES
CLAY	rich in nutrients	slow to warm up in spring (later sowing)
	holds moisture well	difficult to work
	retains nutrients	prone to waterlogging
	less prone to acidity	prone to compaction
SAND	warms up early in spring (earlier sowing)	not very fertile
	easy to work	doesn't hold moisture well
	drains well	doesn't retain nutrients well
	not prone to compaction	prone to acidification
LOAM	good structure	none
	drains well	
	holds moisture	
	retains nutrients well	
PEAT	holds moisture	is often too wet
	often fertile	does not soak up moisture well after having dried out
		warms up slowly in spring
		acid

TYPES OF SOIL

Finding out what type of soil you have in your garden is usually fairly easy. Does the soil stick to your wellies when it's wet but is rock hard in dry conditions? Can you easily press it into a ball in the palm of your hand? Then you're probably dealing with clay. But if it drains quickly and is impossible to make into a ball even when it's wet, then it's probably sand. Clay and sand are extreme soil types, with loam, the third common type of soil, somewhere in the middle. Loam has a crumbly structure with a good mix of small and large particles and it combines the good properties of both clay and sand. The last soil type you might come across is peat soil. Unlike the other soil types, peat is created in bogs where plant remains submerge in water and without the access of air can only partially decompose. Peat soils usually have a dark reddish brown or black colour and a sponge-like structure. They are naturally rather acidic.

SOIL ACIDITY

The acidity or alkalinity of soil is usually expressed as a pH number on a scale from 0 to 14, where 0 means ultra-acidic, 7 neutral and 14 ultra-alkaline. Most vegetables grow best in slightly acidic soils, which translates to a pH between 6 and 7. Very low or high acidity negatively impacts soil life and the availability of nutrients to plants.

To find out the exact pH of your soil, you can have it professionally tested in a laboratory. Or, to get a rough indication, you can buy an inexpensive kit from a garden centre and measure it yourself. There are also many so-called 'indicator' plants that to a trained eye can tell much, not only about the soil's pH but also about its structure and nutrient content.

Acid soil, indicated by a low pH, can be corrected by adding agricultural lime. This is best done over the course of several years, instead of adding a lot of lime at once. Regular application of good compost will increase the humus content of the soil and also help to balance the pH over time. Soils rich in humus are better capable of retaining lime, so a high content of organic matter will help to maintain a more favourable and constant acidity.

It is unfortunately much more difficult to make alkaline soil more acidic – adding lots of (acidic) organic matter such as bark and sawdust can help somewhat, but often your choice of plants will be limited to those that can tolerate alkaline conditions.

Soil improvement

Many years ago I volunteered in a beautiful organic kitchen garden in the south of England. Its only flaw turned out to be the absence of a compost heap. When I asked, with a bucket full of freshly pulled out weeds in hand, where I should empty it, I got a somewhat evasive answer that 'the composting was not really set up properly yet'. It turned out that all organic waste was being thrown down a small hill at the end of the property. What a shame!

By collecting kitchen scraps, weeds, leaves and prunings in a heap and letting them decompose (instead of throwing them down the hill or in the garbage), you can make your own ideal soil improver – for free! No matter the soil type in your garden, compost is a marvellous solution to most of its issues. It not only adds nutrients but, most importantly, it brings a lot of organic matter to the soil. In the compost heap, it is already partially decomposed and will break down further through the action of soil organisms until it turns into humus. Because humus is very stable and only breaks down further if there is no other organic matter available, humus will start to accumulate in the soil. Important characteristics of humus are its capacity to retain water (up to six times its volume) and its ability to hold nutrients. The sticky substance it contains helps soil particles to aggregate, which is how the crumbly structure is formed. In loose, crumbly soil, excessive water can drain freely and plant roots can penetrate easily. By increasing the humus content, you can improve the aeration and drainage of clay, or capacity of sand to hold water and nutrients. There are, of course, more ways to add organic matter to the soil, such as using composted straw-rich manure as a fertiliser or mulching with leaves, straw, grass clippings or cocoa shells. All these materials will eventually be absorbed by the soil and turned into humus. The advantage of compost is that you can easily make it yourself and, because it is already mostly decomposed, it will act faster.

Many soil issues can be remedied by adding compost

COMPOSTING

At the back of my parents' garden is a large patch of vigorous nettles. About twice a year, my father ventures out there and cuts the nettles down to the ground. By then the nettles are almost waist-high and have woody stems. For several years he'd just been adding those nettles to an ever-growing pile in the middle of his little orchard. To him, the pile was an annoying problem that he felt had to be disposed of some day – but how? Then one day he removed the top layer of dried up nettles and uncovered the most beautiful dark and rich compost – the perfect fertiliser for his vegetable patch.

I'm sharing this story to set your mind at ease: composting is in fact a naturally occurring process that doesn't really require you to do anything. If you leave plant waste in a heap for a sufficiently long period of time, it will eventually decompose. However, the process will occur faster and the resulting product will be better if there's a bit of a balance between the so-called brown and green materials. Brown material is dry and rich in carbon (think straw, wood chips, sawdust, twigs and branches), while green material is 'juicy' and rich in nitrogen (grass clippings, annual weeds, spent coffee grounds, kitchen waste). When making a compost heap, follow your intuition: try to alternate between the different materials so that the heap does not become too dry nor too wet. If, for example, you're adding lots of wet, green material such as grass clippings or kitchen waste, try to also add some dry, brown material like straw, wood chips or dry leaves.

Common advice is to turn your compost heap regularly and it's true that it will speed up the composting process. If you do this several times, you could get a finished compost within several weeks. But it is quite laboursome and not necessary: the matter will decompose anyhow. Other, less demanding ways to speed up composting include adding certain plants (comfrey, nettles) or the fermented content of a bokashi bucket. Urine too will aid decomposition and if peeing directly on the compost heap is inconvenient, you can gather urine in a bucket and then pour it over the heap later.

You can set up your composting in different ways – a loose pile is obviously the easiest. But to keep everything somewhat contained, you can also enclose the pile with wire mesh, boards, wood pallets or even straw bales, if you have ample space. In a small urban garden, a compact wooden or plastic bin that can be closed is usually the most practical solution. You can buy bins with a lid on top for adding the waste that also have an opening underneath for taking out the finished compost. The composting process in such bins is relatively slow because the waste is usually added in too small amounts to generate a lot of heat, and also because the pile cannot be turned. The materials you put in will settle and break down so that quite a lot of waste can be added to a single bin over time, but if possible, I recommend having two bins, so that you can fill one completely and leave it to compost while you're filling the second one.

Our current composting system

Because our current kitchen garden is fairly large and because we want to make as much of our own compost as possible, our composting system consists of three compartments enclosed in wooden pallets. Before starting to fill a compartment we line the sides with cardboard. Apart from garden and kitchen waste we also occasionally add some horse manure supplied by our neighbour's brother. The manure adds nutrients to the resulting compost and helps to raise the temperature of the heap, but it is by no means necessary to use it. When one compartment is full, we cover it with another layer of cardboard and start filling the next one. In May I like to plant a single winter squash on top of each finished heap. The plants benefit from the heat created by the composting process and tend to give us many more fruits than plants grown elsewhere in the garden. We do not usually turn our heaps, which means the process takes 6-12 months depending on the time of year, but that is not a problem for us.

CHAPTER 4

No-dig Gardening

Anyone who takes a stroll around allotment gardens on the first warm day of spring will likely encounter several seasoned gardeners dutifully digging over their little patch. Because, as they assure each other, panting from the exertion, 'it has to be done'. Often they are too busy with the heavy labour to stop and ask themselves why they're actually doing it. But if you were to ask, they'd probably say that they're doing it to bury weeds, to incorporate manure and to aerate the soil. And because their father did it too, and his father before him ... and because that's how it should be done!

But why then does everything in nature grow so abundantly even though nobody comes along to 'loosen' the soil? Why is the soil in a forest so beautifully structured even though nobody has dug it over? I've been a no-dig gardener for over 15 years and I know gardeners who've abstained from digging for even longer, some of them on heavy clay. From experience, I can assure you it works: the yields are excellent and our backs are spared. And even when we take over a plot full of weeds, no spades are involved.

The keys to successful no-dig gardening are permanent beds that you do not walk on, and mulch that protects the soil. When you stop digging and leave the soil undisturbed, when you keep it covered with a protective layer of organic mulch, it too will in time become beautifully loose and naturally fertile.

All I need to do in spring is rake the winter mulch aside

10 reasons not to dig

1. NO PROPAGATING PERENNIAL WEEDS

When you dig the soil, the roots of perennial weeds such as couch grass and ground elder are cut into pieces and from every little piece a new plant will grow. Removing every last piece of root is nearly impossible. Covering the soil is much more effective.

2. LESS WEEDS GERMINATING

Soil is full of seeds that are patiently waiting, sometimes for decades, for a chance to sprout. When the soil is dug over, they catch a flash of light which is a signal to germinate. Whenever soil is exposed, nature tries to cover it with plants as quickly as possible to prevent erosion. In undug, undisturbed soil covered with a layer of mulch, seeds remain dormant.

3. PREVENTING BACK INJURIES

Digging is back-breaking labour that can cause back injuries. If you want to burn calories, it's better to find an activity that does not put so much strain on your back.

4. PROTECTING SOIL LIFE

Soil is full of living organisms that all have their specific tasks. When soil is turned over in the course of digging, organisms that live deeper in the soil are exposed to too high levels of oxygen, while soil organisms that live closer to the surface are buried. Every time we dig, we kill many of our helpers and the soil needs time to recover. Digging also disrupts the webs of mycorrhizal fungi which help plants to reach and absorb more nutrients and moisture.

5. REDUCING CO_2 EMISSIONS

When we dig, the carbon in the soil reacts with oxygen from the atmosphere and carbon dioxide (CO_2) is formed. CO_2 is one of the main gasses contributing to the greenhouse effect.

6. LESS WATERING

Undug soil covered with a layer of mulch can absorb moisture better than tilled soil and it is also better at retaining it. That means that much less watering is required.

7. FEEDING SOIL NATURALLY

In nature, organic matter is added to the soil from above – on the surface. Digging in organic fertilisers that are not completely broken down yet can cause a (temporary) nitrogen deficiency. Soil organisms that convert coarse compost with pieces of wood and other materials rich in carbon into humus need nitrogen to do so and will draw the nitrogen from the soil, which means less nitrogen will be available to plants. When (coarse) compost is added to the surface, it will gradually be broken down and absorbed into the soil, but when you dig it in, the decomposition can have negative impact on plant growth in the short term.

8. BETTER SOIL STRUCTURE

Digging, especially when soil is wet or frozen, will not 'aerate' the soil – it will damage soil structure. Surface mulch stimulates the activity of earthworms whose extensive channelling and burrowing can loosen up and aerate even fairly compacted soil.

9. TIME SAVING

Not only does digging take up time, but dug soil requires much more work later on – more weeding and more watering will be necessary. If you do not dig your soil, you'll have more time for the more fun gardening activities such as sowing and harvesting.

10. AN EARLIER START

Instead of digging, in spring I just rake the winter mulch aside and let the soil warm up for a few days, after which I can start sowing or planting. When the soil has been dug over, the growth in spring is slower because the soil life needs time to recover.

Clearance mulch

When establishing a vegetable garden, you'll hardly ever be able to start with weed-free soil, whether you're taking over an allotment garden or sacrificing a part of your lawn. If you're just dealing with some annual weeds, a little hand weeding, hoeing or digging up a few larger plants might be sufficient. But often you'll encounter a problem bigger than that – maybe you're even taking over a garden where persistent perennial weeds were the very reason the previous tenant gave up in desperation. The usual course of action in this case is to dig over the whole plot. That is not only laboursome, but also counterproductive. Next to our previous allotment garden, there was a plot full of the dreaded couch grass. In spring, a new tenant would appear and start by enthusiastically digging the plot over. Within two months, the couch grass grew back with a vengeance. The gardener, not wanting to give up easily, dug the plot over again. But the couch grass always showed more persistence and after two seasons at most, the gardener threw in the towel and gave up gardening because it turned out to be so much hard work.

Luckily, there is a much more effective way to tackle an overgrown garden and it does not put a strain on your back either: clearance mulch. The principle is simple: in order to grow, all plants need light and if you take the light away, they die. That means that if you cover an overgrown plot with a material that excludes light, all weeds will eventually perish. My preferred material for this is cardboard since it is a free resource and unlike landscape plastic for example, it allows water and air to permeate and the soil life underneath to thrive.

You can start covering your garden anytime you wish, but since the mulch is only effective when plants are actively growing, count on having to leave the mulch in place for a whole growing season. If you cover the soil before

Cardboard excludes light, eventually killing the weeds underneath

winter, the mulch (cardboard) will start to break down, but will not be doing much good yet, since plants are not really growing at that time. The best time in our climate is around March, after the soil has already warmed up a bit, but plants are only just beginning to grow. Covering the soil does not mean you won't be able to grow anything for a year, but you will be limited in your plant choice during the first season. Carrots, for example, which need to be sown directly and have a deep tap root are better left for later. The best plants for the first season are those with rampant growth that will cover a large area. One winter squash plant, with its trailing growth habit, will cover about three square metres for which you only need to make one hole in the mulch to plant it. Every hole in the mulch presents an opportunity for the weeds underneath to grow through, so it is best to make as few as possible. Other vegetables to consider for the first season are courgettes and other summer squash, cucumbers, tomatoes and potatoes.

WEED-FREE SOIL IN FIVE STEPS

1. Mow or trample any tall plants

You can mow any tall plants and leave them on the ground or you can simply trample them. If the vegetation is low (for example if you are starting with a lawn) you don't need to do anything.

2. Add organic fertiliser

This is an optional step, but especially if the soil is not very fertile and poorly structured, it's a good idea to add some organic matter right away. The best materials to use are homemade compost or composted manure – horse or cow manure is best. This way you'll also stimulate soil life. It does not matter if the compost or manure you're using is full of weed seeds (which it often is) because even if the seeds germinate, they won't be able to penetrate the cardboard and will die.

3. Cover the plot with cardboard

Cardboard will exclude light which means the plants underneath will die. Large pieces of cardboard are preferable, such as those used for packaging of furniture or (since we live in the Netherlands) bikes. Try to look for cardboard with little print, but most inks these days are plant-based and black ink in particular shouldn't be a problem. Remove any tape or staples. Lay the pieces down, overlapping them by at least 30 centimetres. Weigh the cardboard down so that it does not blow away. We use miscellaneous tiles, stones and bricks for this. If you are planning on adding another layer (step 4), you don't have to do this.

4. Add a layer of weed-free organic material

This step too is optional, but it will disguise the cardboard so it can be handy if you're using this method in a place where a field of cardboard would not be appreciated. It is important to only use materials that do not contain weed seed, which excludes most homemade compost. We usually use mushroom compost or municipal compost for beds and woodchip to mark the paths. However, I have found that topping the cardboard with organic matter will usually make it break down faster and therefore possibly less effective.

5. Plant through the cardboard

Use a trowel to make a small hole in the cardboard through which you can plant a pre-sown vegetable plant. You might want to add a bit of compost too. Try to make as few holes as possible and use plants that will spread, such as winter squash. If the composting process underneath the cardboard causes temporary nitrogen deficiency (your plants will look pale and stunted), use a liquid fertiliser to add some quickly available nitrogen (e.g. diluted urine or fermented nettle fertiliser).

Winter squash planted through the cardboard

Some favourite squashes, including butternut, delicata, spaghetti, mini-pumpkins, hubbard and naked seeded pumpkins

A FEW OF MY FAVOURITE WINTER SQUASHES

Since we want to be as self-sufficient as possible and do not have a freezer (one of the most energy-hungry household appliances), winter squash that can be stored without refrigeration for many months is an important crop for us. Years of using the above method to eliminate weeds in different gardens have given me the opportunity to grow numerous varieties of winter squash. Out of these unofficial trials, several favourites have emerged. When space allows, I like to grow all of the squashes mentioned below because they are all quite different and lend themselves to various preparations in the kitchen. In general, I prefer smaller-fruited 'one-meal squash' to those producing huge fruits. The giants might win you awards at a vegetable show, but are rather impractical in the kitchen.

I start my plants about three weeks before our average frost date and plant them out about four to five weeks later when the nights are also warm enough. After the harvest I cure the fruits on a sunny windowsill for about 10 days, after which we store them in our unheated bedroom in crates under our bed.

Spaghetti squash (*Cucurbita pepo*)

When you cook or bake this type of squash (also called 'vegetable spaghetti'), the flesh falls apart into spaghetti-like strands. It has become popular as a low-carb substitute for pasta (even though the taste is nothing like real spaghetti) and I too like to serve it with tomato-based sauces. There are several different varieties out of which 'Small Wonder' is my favourite because of its handy size. Spaghetti squash keeps for about three to six months.

Delicata squash (*Cucurbita pepo*)

The pretty cylindrical fruits are ivory coloured with green stripes and their delicate skin means there's no need to peel them. I like them best cut in ½in rounds and simply roasted. The taste is reminiscent of sweet potato. Delicata keeps for three to six months.

Butternut squash (*Cucurbita moschata*)

My absolute favourite squash and the one I'd grow if I only had space for one variety. The seed cavity is small, so there's a lot of usable sweet flesh. Butternuts are very versatile in the kitchen and I often roast one on Sunday and then use it for different dishes such as soups, gnocchi and cakes. Butternuts require quite a lot of warmth, but 'Harrier', a British-bred variety especially selected for cool summers, has performed consistently well with us. They keep for about nine months.

Hubbard squash (*Cucurbita maxima*)

Hubbard squash has lemon-shaped fruits and orange flesh rich in carotene. Because of their excellent chestnut-like taste and because they keep well in storage, they are rightfully some of the most popular winter squashes. There are many varieties but because of their smaller size my favourites are 'Baby Blue Hubbard' (grey) and 'Uchiki Kuri' (orange). I like to use them in soups or cut them into wedges and roast them. They keep throughout the winter.

Mini-pumpkins (*Cucurbita pepo*)

Out of the varieties available, I have grown 'Jack-be-Little', 'Gold Speck' (both bright orange) and 'Baby Boo' (white) which produce a large number of tiny fruits, about 8cm (3in) in diameter. Their cuteness makes them perfect for decorating your house for fall and when you get tired of your décor, you can eat them! Because of the small size of the fruits, these varieties are also perfect for climbing up a tipi or a fence. You can stuff them with various fillings and bake them in the oven. They keep for up to six months, but are best used within three months.

Naked seeded pumpkins (*Cucurbita pepo*)

Even though the flesh of these pumpkins is edible, they are nowhere near as tasty as the other varieties I mentioned. They are also not grown for their flesh but for their hull-less seeds. The two varieties I have grown are 'Kakai' and 'Penelopa' (a spawn of 'Gleisdorfer' grown commercially in Austria), out of which the second one had bigger fruits and gave us an overall bigger harvest of seeds. Even though this is not a squash I'd grow if space was limited, the fresh seeds are delicious.

Naked seeded pumpkin

I created this dish as a vegetarian option for a festive fall dinner with the mini-pumpkins from our garden. The stuffed pumpkins not only look cute but can also be prepped in advance, which makes this dish perfect for fall entertaining – anything from a harvest festival to Thanksgiving.

Stuffed mini-pumpkins

- 8 mini-pumpkins of about 8cm diameter
- 160g (1 cup) wild rice
- 1 red onion, finely chopped
- 2 tbsp olive oil
- 1 clove of garlic, finely chopped
- 1 tbsp of chopped thyme, sage, rosemary (any or all) + a few whole sprigs
- 30g (¼ cup) dried cranberries
- 50g (½ cup) walnuts or pecans, roughly chopped
- 2 tangerines, juice of
- Salt, pepper
- ½ tsp ground cinnamon

Put the wild rice in a medium saucepan and add enough water to cover by about 2cm (¾in). Add salt and bring to a boil. Simmer the rice until it is al dente, about 30 minutes. Drain any residual water. Meanwhile, cut the tops off pumpkins (reserve those for later). Using a large spoon, scoop out seeds and strings. Brush the inside, the outside and the tops with a bit of olive oil.

Preheat the oven to 190°C (375°F).

In a large pan, heat the olive oil and bake the onion with a pinch of salt until slightly caramelised, about 10-15 minutes. Add the garlic and sauté for a minute more. Add the rest of the ingredients and season to taste. Stir well and take off the heat.

Fill the prepared pumpkins with the stuffing and cover with the pumpkin lids. Place the pumpkins in a casserole pan and tuck in a few sprigs of herbs around them. Put the lid on and bake in the preheated oven for about 45 minutes, until the pumpkins can easily be pierced with a knife and are slightly golden around the edges.

Several possible layouts for a small kitchen garden measuring 3 x 5m (3yd 1ft x 5yd 1ft)

Gardening in raised beds

Once your soil is free of weeds, it's time to determine the layout of your garden. Because most of the plants in the kitchen garden are annuals, it is theoretically possible to change your layout every year. But if you do not intend to dig, it is best to create permanent beds. This way you'll never walk on the soil, it will not become compacted and it won't be necessary to loosen it repeatedly. In addition, when you work with permanent raised beds, you can apply manure and mulch exactly where they are needed instead of wasting materials by applying them to the whole plot. What shape you give your beds depends on your personal preferences, but my advice would be to seek a happy balance between the aesthetic and the practical. A kitchen garden laid out as a labyrinth might look fun on paper but will be less amusing once you have to navigate a fully loaded wheelbarrow over the winding paths.

Personally, I'm a fan of simple geometrical layouts and our garden is divided into long rectangular beds. Rectangular beds are easier to construct and maintain and straight paths are practical in a garden where you'll constantly be walking back and forth. And since most plots are rectangular, straight beds usually make a good use of the available space. Long rectangular beds are by no means your only option though – you can play with other shapes too, but do try to keep the layout relatively simple. And if a geometrical layout seems too rigid to you, don't forget that once the beds are overflowing with colourful vegetables, the impression will be very different. The layout is but a canvas onto which you paint a beautiful new artwork every year with vegetables, herbs and edible flowers.

In order to be able to reach the whole surface of your beds from the path comfortably, they shouldn't be too wide. A width of 120cm

(4ft) works well for most people, but I also know a very tall gardener who makes his beds 150cm (5ft) wide. On the other hand, where children are involved in gardening, it's better to make the beds narrower, say 90-100cm (around 3ft). Do not make the beds too long either because then having to walk around them might become annoying – I make mine around 3m (10ft) long.

The paths between the beds should be at least 30cm (1ft), but make them twice as wide (60cm/2ft) if you want to be able to comfortably manoeuvre a wheelbarrow. At first sight it will probably seem that the paths take up a large portion of the space, but because the beds can be planted up intensively, this system in fact makes a much better use of the space than the traditional growing in long rows that you need to be able to walk between.

DIFFERENT KINDS OF RAISED BEDS

Because you'll be walking on the paths, the soil there will get compacted, while your beds will get taller because you'll be topping them with manure and mulch. Over time, a difference in height between paths and beds will naturally occur. You can choose to accentuate this difference by constructing a frame around your beds and filling it up with more material. Raised beds have numerous advantages: they give your garden a defined structure and improve drainage. Because the soil in a raised bed dries and warms up faster in spring, you can start sowing earlier. In the course of my gardening career, I have tried different kinds of raised beds, which each have their pros and cons.

No frame beds

The easiest and cheapest solution is a raised bed without a frame – as I said earlier, a difference in height between a path and a bed will occur naturally and become more pronounced over time. But in my experience, without a frame to keep it in place, mulch will spread onto the paths and make them narrower and narrower. In the end more upkeep is often necessary to maintain the beds than if they had been framed to start with.

Different types of raised beds each have their pros and cons

Wooden frames

Wooden frames in combination with woodchip covered paths are, in my opinion, the most practical option that requires the least upkeep. However, wood can be expensive and will not last as long as concrete tiles will. Of the trees grown locally, the wood of Douglas pine and larch is the most rot-resistant. It is also possible to use recycled wood as long as it has not been treated with harmful substances that could leach into the soil. For our raised beds we use Douglas fir boards 15cm (6in) wide and 2.2cm (almost 1in) thick, which we simply screw together in the corners. Sometimes we first treat the wood with organic linseed oil based paint in order to increase its durability. I use a light blue colour that I have custom-mixed and which sets off the green of the plants nicely. Our oldest (treated) beds are now onto their eighth season and are still functional. We have moved gardens twice in the meantime and the beds were easy to transport – the two of us can simply pick up a frame and carry it to its new location. To increase their lifespan, we turned the frames upside down when moving them – this way the bottom part that is in contact with soil and therefore more exposed to moisture, comes up on top. The lifespan of wooden frames depends, of course, largely on the kind of wood you use: thicker boards made of hardwood such as oak would last even longer but also cost a lot more.

Concrete tiles frames

A concrete sidewalk tile on its side, partially dug into the soil, makes an easy to construct and extremely durable frame for a raised bed. This works especially well if your paths are made of tiles too, because the upright tiles will be stabilised by the tile paths on one side and the soil which fills the bed on the other. The tiles used most often for sidewalks and terraces around here are a handy 30 x 30cm (1 x 1ft). Which means four next to each other will make a 120cm (4ft) wide bed, one row laid horizontally will make a 30cm (1ft) wide path and a double row a 60cm (2ft) path which is ideal for a wheelbarrow. All the tiles we've ever used we got for free, sometimes we found them in our neighbourhood, sometimes online. People putting in a new terrace are usually only too glad when you offer to relieve them of the discarded tiles. Constructing the beds is quite laboursome but they last forever. As always, it is important to start with soil free of perennial weeds but even so, you'll have to remove some weeds that germinate between the tiles from time to time.

Another drawback is that the soil close to the edges tends to dry out a bit more and sometimes ants will make a nest there. Other recycled building materials such as bricks and roofing tiles can be used for constructing raised beds too.

Tiles are free and durable but the soil close to the edges tends to dry out a bit

Mulching

Mulching means nothing more or less than covering the soil, but in my opinion it is THE key to a low-maintenance garden. A clearance mulch (which I described previously, see page 63) can be used at an early stage to get rid of weeds in an overgrown garden. But later, after perennial weeds have been subdued, a maintenance mulch of various organic materials will prevent the ever-present weed seeds from sprouting. Even if the seeds manage to germinate, the seedlings will usually get exhausted before they'll be able to penetrate the mulch layer. A permanent cover of organic material that slowly decomposes also means that we are continuously adding nutrients to the soil and that the amount of humus in soil is increasing. Moreover, mulch protects the soil from drying out which means watering need not be as frequent. Mulch also prevents erosion by protecting soil from being washed away in a rainstorm. All in all, a layer of mulch keeps the soil in good condition and improves and protects soil structure. Besides, if we do not cover the soil, nature will do so by quickly sprouting weeds in order to protect the precious topsoil. And that in turn will keep us very busy!

It is important to keep in mind that mulch will conserve the current condition of the soil. This means that it is best to wait till the soil is moist and has warmed up before applying it, instead of mulching soil that is cold or dry. During the winter months, mulch will protect the soil from the elements and in spring, when you want to start sowing, you can simply rake the mulch to the side and let the soil warm up. This way you create an instant seedbed with a fine structured soil. After your seeds have sprouted, you can add a layer of suitable mulch material around the young plants. Plants started in pots can simply be planted through the layer of mulch. Relatively large seeds such as broad beans, French beans and peas can also be sown directly into the mulch.

If slugs are a problem in your garden, you might want to stick to mulching with already mostly decomposed materials such as mushroom compost and communal compost which are relatively fine structured. We garden in a wet climate however, and contrary to what is often maintained, it is not my experience that mulching significantly increases slug problems. Though our garden is definitely not slug free, they do not seem to be causing more damage than in surrounding gardens where no mulch is used. We accidentally had the opportunity to test the effect of mulch last year when our neighbours decided to forego any mulching because of the slug damage they had experienced in the previous year. We both planted pre-sown broad beans of the same variety at the same time, but unlike their bed, ours was immediately mulched with partially decomposed straw. At first, our plants exhibited slightly more slug damage, but they quickly recovered and grew stronger and produced longer than our neighbours' plants, even though our neighbours watered their plants more frequently. My hunch is that the positive effects of mulching outweigh the possible initial setback. Moreover, mulch creates a habitat for slug predators such as ground beetles and centipedes, which in turn will also help to keep the slug population in check.

Applying a layer of mulch in spring will save you a lot of work later in the season

MULCH MATERIALS

Many different organic materials can be used for mulching, but their specific properties make them suited to different situations and different crops. Because the chemical composition and nutrient content differs, it is a good idea to vary the mulch you use, instead of using the same materials over and over, in order to provide a varied diet for the soil organisms.

Cocoa shells

Cocoa shells are the husk of cocoa beans, in other words they are the waste product of the chocolate industry. Even though cocoa is grown far away, the beans are usually only processed after transportation. Since most of the beans come to Europe through the port of Amsterdam, this waste product is in fact created locally. Cocoa shells are rich in nutrients and every time it rains, some nutrients are released and become available to plants. The delicious chocolate scent helps to confuse pests and slugs do not like to crawl over the rough shells. But beware: cocoa is toxic to dogs, so you might want to refrain from using cocoa shells as mulch in gardens where dogs are present. The biggest drawback of cocoa shells is their price that has at least doubled since we've started using them. I therefore use them sparingly and reserve them for plants that attract a lot of pests and/or are especially susceptible to slug damage.

Straw

Garden centres sell bags of straw to be used as bedding for small animals such as hamsters,

but for mulching your garden it is usually more profitable to buy whole bales from a farmer. Organically grown straw is preferable since non-organic can have been sprayed with herbicides that might negatively impact the growth of your plants. Straw is too coarse a material to use for mulching delicate plants, but it is well suited for larger vegetables such as courgettes and tomatoes. Traditionally, it has been used for mulching strawberries to protect the fruits from rotting and it will do the same for fruiting vegetables – pumpkins lying on a layer of straw are less prone to rot.

Grass clippings

If you have a lawn, even a small one, you'll have no shortage of grass clippings. If you don't, you can probably get some from your neighbours who'll be only too happy to get rid of their 'waste'. Of course, you should only use grass clippings from gardens where no inorganic fertilisers, herbicides or pesticides are used. Grass clippings are best spread in a relatively thin layer, since a thick layer could cause an anaerobic process (rotting) and turn the grass into a slimy mess. Grass clippings are high in nitrogen and can be used around just about any vegetable.

Leaves

A layer of leaves that falls on the ground in autumn is nature's own way of mulching. You can rake leaves away from places where you don't want them (terrace, paths, lawn and the sidewalk) and use them as mulch around perennial plants. In the kitchen garden, I use them in autumn to cover beds that are empty or still contain some overwintering vegetables like Brussels sprouts and kale. If the leaves are dry, they get easily blown away by wind, which is why I like to put wire mesh on top in the beginning, until the leaves get wet and start decomposing. Leaves from different species of trees differ in acidity and nutrient content, which is why it is a good idea to vary the source of your leaves. There is also a difference in how fast leaves will decompose – the leaves of beech and oak will decompose relatively quickly, other species will take longer. The leaves of both English and black walnut (*Juglans regia* and *J. nigra*) are best avoided since they contain juglone, an allelopathic chemical that can negatively impact the growth of some plants.

Compost

Because a small compost pile usually does not heat up enough to kill all pathogens and weed seeds, using homemade compost as mulch is often problematic. A possible solution is a two-layer mulch: first a layer of compost (or composted manure), then another layer of weed-free material such as straw. The top layer stops any weed seeds that might sprout from the compost or manure – they'll get exhausted by having to grow through the additional mulch layer.

Then there is municipal compost – because it is composted in large quantities, high temperatures are generated and the compost is usually free of weed seeds. In some municipalities here residents can pick up a load in spring for free, in others they have to pay for the compost. In contrast to homemade compost, you never know exactly what you're getting – the quality is variable and apart from pieces of plastic, the compost might also contain herbicide residues.

Mushroom compost

Mushroom compost is the substrate on which mushrooms were grown, consisting mostly of horse manure, gypsum, chicken manure and straw. After the mushrooms have been harvested, the substrate is heated to 70°C (160°F), which kills all pathogens and weed seeds. Because of the addition of gypsum, mushroom compost is usually alkaline, making it suitable for acidic soils. On the other hand, if your soil already is alkaline, repeated use of mushroom compost is not a good idea. Fresh mushroom compost is light brown and has a fibrous texture, whereas mushroom compost that has been weathered is dark and has a crumbly structure. My favourite is weathered mushroom compost from organic mushroom farms but it is not always easy to find.

Woodchip

Anyone who has trees in their yard is likely to end up with lots of twigs and branches from pruning them. One solution is to chop those up and use as mulch. Because wood is rich in carbon it causes a temporary nitrogen deficiency in the soil when it decomposes and this makes it less suitable for growing annual vegetables. However, since this effect is mostly limited to close to the surface of the soil where the woodchip is decomposing, plants with deeper roots will not be so affected. So if you pre-sow your plants and only set them out after they have a well-established root system, they will probably be fine. Likewise, vegetables from the legumes family that are able to use atmospheric nitrogen are not affected – our neighbours once had a very good crop of broad beans in a bed mulched with woodchip. Nevertheless, in my own garden I tend to use woodchip mainly for paths and around perennial plants, especially fruiting bushes.

Plant remains

Even weeds make good mulch, provided they have not formed seeds yet. Just pull them out and leave them on the soil surface between your vegetables. The best time to do this is on a warm sunny day when they will wilt quickly. You can also mulch with any parts of vegetables that you do not use in the kitchen. I especially like to use the large leaves of rhubarb, which, unlike the stalks, are not edible.

Coffee grounds

Few nations enjoy coffee as much as the Dutch do, so even though we only collect coffee grounds from family members, we have a pretty good supply. If your family prefers tea, you could try collecting coffee grounds from a coffee shop. Coffee grounds are rich in nutrients, have an almost ideal pH of 6.5-6.8 and worms love them too. If that is not enough to convince you to start using them in your garden, know that they also make a good slug barrier. Last year when our carrot seedlings were getting decimated, I applied a layer of coffee grounds around them and it did the trick.

Caring for your garden throughout the growing season

WATERING

All plants need water to thrive – annual vegetables more than perennials since they do not get the time to develop an equally extensive root system. In a permaculture vegetable garden we are already doing a lot to reduce the necessity of watering: our undug soil is better at holding moisture, while mulch reduces evaporation. But in long periods of dry weather, we too will need to water the garden. Soft (rain) water is best for your plants, so try to use every opportunity to catch and store it. In our garden we catch the water from our little shed and store it in rain butts. However, the surface area of our shed's roof is too small to provide all the water our garden needs, which is why we had a borehole drilled in the garden. It is equipped with a simple water pump that gives us a good workout. Groundwater is cold and plants do not enjoy that, so we always fill two rain butts and let the water warm up before we use it for watering. The next time we want to water, it is at optimum temperature.

The best time for watering is early morning or in the evening, but if you water in the evening, try to avoid getting the plants wet, since that could lead to fungal disease. When watering tomatoes especially, water the soil and avoid wetting the leaves, in order to prevent blight (*Phytophtora*). A substantial watering once a week is better than watering a little every day because it stimulates the plant's roots to grow deeper. A good heavy watering comes down to about 10-20 litres per square metre (2.2-4.4 gallons per square yard), less if your soil is clay and more if it is sandy.

Apart from this general rule, there are certain cases when you need to be especially vigilant:

After sowing – seeds need water in order to germinate and a seedbed should be kept moist until the seeds sprout. In dry conditions you can use this little trick: draw a drill with the pointed side of a trowel and moisten it thoroughly. Place the seeds in the drill and cover them with dry soil – the dry soil seals in the moisture.

After planting out – until the plants root properly, they should be watered regularly.

Fruiting vegetables – all vegetables that we grow for their fruits and seeds (tomatoes, beans, peas) need a lot of water when they're flowering in order to set a lot of fruits. However, when the fruit of tomatoes start swelling, it is better to water less so that the flavour is not diluted and fruits do not split and crack.

Leafy vegetables – regular watering is necessary to ensure tender leaves and prevent premature bolting.

A LITTLE EXTRA FOR YOUR PLANTS

Through taking good care of your soil, adding lots of organic material and mulching, you're well on your way to an abundant garden. As long as you take good care of your soil, it should provide most of the nutrients your crops will need. But especially on light sandy soils, such as mine, or in the early stages of a garden, heavy feeders such as cabbages and squash might need a little extra. Every year, at the beginning of summer, I make a big batch of fermented liquid fertiliser. The two plants most commonly used for this are nettles (rich in nitrogen) or comfrey (rich in potassium) – I like to use a mix of both for a reasonably balanced product. It is also possible to ferment other plants and make liquids for specific applications. For example, common horsetail (*Equisetum arvense*), which is rich in silicon, can be used to strengthen plant cell walls and prevent fungal diseases, and dandelion (*Taraxacum officinale*) supports healthy growth and improves the quality of fruits. Personally, I do not usually intervene if I notice my plants are under attack from pests – I prefer to wait until natural predators appear and restore the balance. But in desperate times you can try spraying your plants with fermented rhubarb leaves or tansy (*Tanacetum vulgare*).

Fermented liquid feed recipe

Fill a barrel or a rain butt two-thirds with plants cut into 10-20cm (4-8in) pieces. Top the plants with water but not quite to the brim, since the mixture will bubble up a little. If you just want to make a small batch, use about 1kg (2lb) of plant material to 10 litres (2.5 gallons) of water. Stir the contents occasionally.

The fermenting plants will become quite smelly. I have come to associate the scent with gardening and have actually grown almost fond of it, but if you find it too penetrating, you can add a handful of basalt rock dust to bind the odour. The feed is finished when the fermentation stops – in summer it takes about 10-15 days, during the colder months longer. The resulting product is quite potent and needs to be diluted with water. If you're using it on the soil, dilute it at a 1:10 ratio; if you're spraying it on the plants' leaves, dilute at 1:20.

CHAPTER 5

Smart Growing

Deciding what to grow

Now that you have improved the soil and prepared your garden beds, it's time to decide what you'll fill them with. Obviously, the most important thing is to grow what you enjoy eating, because even though snow peas are one of the easiest vegetables to grow and very productive, there's no point in growing a whole bed of them if you don't like them. Every year before ordering any seeds, I ask for input from all family members. Taking into account their preferences means that more vegetables will be eaten in our home and that, of course, is why I grow vegetables in the first place. By now, I know that growing sweet corn and sugar snap peas is a must and that crispy romaine lettuces will be met with more enthusiasm than loose-leaf varieties.

Sweet corn

Purple sugar snap peas

But apart from you and your beloveds' personal preferences, there are other factors to take into consideration when choosing your crops. Is this your first vegetable garden and would you like to grow something relatively easy with a high probability of success? Or is your aim to grow specialty produce not easily found in a store? Is self-sufficiency your dream? Or is your garden tiny and are you looking for ways to obtain the biggest possible yield from a limited space?

In the overview overleaf you'll find suggestions for vegetables from different categories. Naturally, in many cases the categories will overlap - courgette, for example, is easy to grow, high yielding and mini-courgettes with flowers attached are expensive to buy.

Bear in mind that these recommendations are based on our climate and while a lot of my advice is universal, some may be mostly relevant to gardeners growing vegetables under similar conditions. If your climate is sunnier and drier, tomatoes, for example might be easy to grow and very productive, while in our rainy summers they are plagued by blight.

REAR

Chard

1. EASY TO GROW

These vegetables will almost always do well and are not too demanding as far as growing conditions are concerned. They have few pest or disease problems and are therefore ideal for the beginner gardener who wants to build up some self-confidence, or for gardeners who have very little time to spend on their plot.

- Beets, chard, lettuce, winter purslane, beans, peas, endive, courgette, tomatillo, radishes.

2. HIGH YIELDING

These vegetables give the highest yield in proportion to the amount of space they take up and the time they spend in the ground. For example, cut-and-come-again leaves can usually be harvested about three times, the first time just four or five weeks after sowing. Vegetables that can be grown vertically and thus don't take up much space on the ground score well too.

- Cut-and-come-again salad leaves (rocket, mustard greens, lettuce), broccoli rabe, all climbing beans and peas, courgette, early potatoes, early beets (sown thickly and harvested small), fast-growing Oriental brassicas (such as tatsoi and pak choi), early carrots.

3. EXPENSIVE

The high price of vegetables is often caused by the cost of harvesting – if something needs to be harvested manually and/or extra carefully, it will be expensive to buy. It does not necessarily mean that these vegetables are difficult to grow though! In other cases, the price is a function of scarcity – vegetables that are little grown and not much of which is sold will be expensive too.

- Snow peas (mangetout), sugar snaps, shallots, mixed leaves, corn salad (lamb's lettuce), asparagus, mini-pumpkins, edible flowers.

4. UNBUYABLES

In a way, everything you grow falls into this category – the absolute freshness of homegrown produce is something that you simply cannot buy. But many vegetables or varieties are not grown commercially at all. Sometimes these are little known vegetables, other times it is an unusual variety of a well-known crop. Here are some edibles that we cannot buy where we live:

- Fresh borlotti beans, fresh gherkins, tomatillos, yellow snow peas, summer purslane, colourful kale, most edible flowers, many Oriental greens (tatsoi).

5. BETTER FRESH

Very fresh vegetables are usually sweeter than vegetables that have been harvested days ago (i.e. just about everything you buy in a shop), because from the moment of harvest, the sugars start to convert to starch. The most striking example of this is probably old-fashioned varieties of sweet corn, which you should only harvest after you've got your water boiling. Here are a few examples that taste considerably better when freshly harvested:

- Asparagus, sweet corn, peas, early carrots, green beans, lettuce.

Fresh gherkins

Harvest bowls are something I like to make on Sundays, when we come home with a basket overflowing with fresh produce. They are a way to showcase what we're harvesting at a certain point in the year, a way to celebrate the changing seasons in the garden. I like to include different types of vegetables (root, fruit, leaf) prepared in a variety of ways (raw, roasted, boiled, fermented, grilled). The base is usually a wholegrain, and there is usually some protein source and a sauce to go on top. Here is a seasonal example, but it is meant more as an inspiration than a recipe to follow to the letter.

Winter harvest bowl

Boiled wholegrain rice

TOFU:

375g (13oz) firm tofu, in 8mm (⅓in) slices
3 tbsp soy sauce
2 tbsp sesame seed oil
Pinch of chilli flakes
1 garlic clove, minced
½ lime, juice of

ROASTED VEGETABLES:

500g (1lb) beetroot
1 delicata squash (or other winter squash)
500g (1lb) parsnips
4 tbsp olive oil
2 tbsp balsamic vinegar
Salt, black pepper

OTHER VEGETABLES:

2 large carrots
Mix of hardy salad leaves (winter purslane, corn salad, land cress)
Sauerkraut

SAUCE:

60ml (¼ cup) tahini
½ lemon, juice of
3 tbsp water
½ tsp ground turmeric

Preheat the oven to 200°C (400°F). Put the sliced tofu in a shallow wide bowl. Mix soy sauce with sesame seed oil, chilli flakes, garlic and lime juice and pour the marinade over the tofu slices. Let sit while you prepare the other vegetables.

Cut beetroot into wedges and toss with 2 tbsp of olive oil and the balsamic vinegar. Season with salt and pepper. Cut the squash in half, scoop out the seeds and cut into half-rounds. Toss with 1 tbsp oil and season well. Cut the parsnips in batons, toss with the remaining tablespoon of olive oil and season.

Arrange vegetables in a single layer on one or two baking sheets (keep the beetroot separate so that it does not stain the other vegetables). Spread the marinated tofu on a baking sheet as well. Put the baking sheets in the preheated oven. Bake 10 minutes, then turn the tofu slices and toss the vegetables. Bake for another 10 minutes. The tofu, squash and parsnips will probably be done; the beetroot might need 5-10 minutes more.

Meanwhile, grate the carrots coarsely and dress with a bit of olive oil and a good squeeze of lemon juice. In a small bowl, mix all ingredients for the sauce together.

To serve, put a serving of rice in a shallow bowl. Arrange the tofu, roasted and other vegetables on top and finish with a drizzle of the tahini sauce and a sprinkling of pumpkin seeds on top.

Maximising the use of space

Having gone to all the trouble of improving your soil and constructing permanent raised beds, you'll undoubtedly want to use them as efficiently as possible and there are different ways to maximise the productivity of your garden.

To start with, it is important to align the amount of vegetables you sow or plant with your needs. The gardener who's giving away countless lettuces and kilos of courgettes every summer is undoubtedly a blessing for his gardenless surroundings, but will probably be harvesting little from his garden a few months later. The garden of most people is not large enough for complete self-sufficiency, and it is a pity if short bursts of abundance are periodically followed by long periods of famine.

Some years ago I heard about a dedicated gardener who grew large amounts of a few kinds of vegetables and stored her harvest in the freezer. The whole year she kept to a strict schedule of eating beets on Mondays, kale on Tuesdays, broad beans on Wednesdays and so on. But the prospect of eating the same vegetables year in year out does not excite me and would not be a reason for me to start a garden – in that case you might as well buy your vegetables from the freezer section at a grocery store! For me, the reason to sow and plant every year again is the pleasure of a varied diet that follows the seasons and of eating every crop at its absolute best. This does not mean that various ways of preserving and storing your harvest for the leaner months are not a good idea – I too make tomatillo chutney when the harvest is overwhelming. But it is important to strive for a continuous supply of fresh vegetables instead of always having either too much or too little.

CONTINUOUS SOWING

One of the things you can do to spread your harvest is to sow small amounts of seeds several times during the season instead of sowing a whole seed package at once. If, for example, you want to be harvesting tender young beets for months, you can first sow a few rows at the beginning of April and then repeat the sowing every 3-4 weeks till the end of June. You can harvest the beets about 12 weeks after sowing and because you will be harvesting them small, the rows can be spaced closer together – about 15-20cm (6-8in).

Another handy little trick is to replant some of your direct-sown seedlings after they come up – the replanted seedlings will mature slower than those that were left in place. This works especially well with lettuce: you sow a row and when it's time to thin, you replant some of the seedlings into a new row. Moving the seedlings will temporarily stunt the growth, which means that the replanted lettuce will be ready for harvest a couple of weeks later. So even if you only sow once, you can avoid your lettuce bolting because you cannot possibly eat 20 heads in a week! In a similar way you can spread the harvest of endive and kohlrabi, for example.

Of course, not everything can be planned and you can't control the weather either. An especially cold and rainy summer or a long period of draught can cause a crop to fail completely. On the other hand, it can also happen that something will grow so well that you will end up with a surplus no matter how carefully you calculated your needs. In that case, enjoy and share the bounty!

SUCCESSIONAL PLANTING

Making good use of the available space also means preventing vegetable beds from ever being empty. Most vegetables will only occupy the ground for a part of the growing season and that means that beside the main crop you can often squeeze in an early crop or a late one after the main crop has been harvested. When you know that a courgette will not be planted out before mid-May, you can sow spinach or radishes first. And in September, when the courgette plant is mostly finished, you can still sow a few rows of winter purslane or corn salad. With most vegetables, you can also limit the time they will spend in the ground by pre-sowing them in pots or modules instead of sowing directly into a bed. For example, if you sow kale in modules, you will be planting the seedlings out 4-6 weeks later, which means the space will remain available for a different crop 4-6 weeks longer. To gain even more time, you can often overlap different crops within one bed. To go back to the aforementioned courgette: if you have sown spinach in a bed where you want to plant courgette around mid-May, you do not need to pull all the spinach out before you do so. At this moment, the courgette plant is not very big and it suffices to just take out some spinach in the middle of the bed in order to plant it. The more the courgette grows, the more spinach will be pulled out, until the courgette completely takes over the space. An added bonus is that the soil will continuously be protected by a cover of plants. You can see more possibilities of including early and late crops in Chapter 6.

EARLY CROP	**MAIN CROP**	**LATE CROP**
radishes	cucumber	corn salad
mustard greens	tomatoes	winter purslane
rocket	sweet corn	rocket
snow peas & sugar snaps	courgette	broad beans (*OW*)
spinach	beans	chervil
broad beans	chard	Belgian endive
peas	kale	garlic (*OW*)
early potatoes	maincrop potatoes	oriental radishes
lettuce	aubergine	fennel
	broccoli	spinach
		OW = over wintering

Sweet corn interplanted with chard

This is just an indication of what category the different crops fall into. The time they will spend in the ground differs within each category too. Radishes for example, can be harvested and make room for a second crop much earlier than broad beans or early potatoes. On the other hand, if you want to, you can usually keep harvesting chard and kale well into fall but in that case you will not be able to plant a follow-up crop.

INTERCROPPING

Vegetables that need to be planted relatively far apart, and/or are very slow to grow, can be interplanted with another crop in order to maximise the yield from the given space. A good example is sweet corn, which needs to be planted at least 30cm (12in) apart in both directions, but because of its upright growing habit does not cover the soil. This means that you can intercrop it with another low-growing vegetable: I usually choose lettuce or chard. An additional advantage of combining these two crops is that corn will protect the leaf vegetables from too much sun during the warmest months, preventing them from bolting prematurely. Meanwhile, the lettuce or chard will keep the soil covered and will prevent weed growth and excessive evaporation.

In a similar way, you can use the space under a bean tipi. I make a bean tipi from six to eight long bamboo canes arranged in a circle and tied together at the top. Two seeds are sown next to every cane, but before the beans completely cover the tipi, the space underneath it can be used for lettuce or fast-growing Oriental brassicas, for example.

Sometimes you can intersperse rows of a slow-growing crop with a fast-growing one. Parsnips need to be sown in April but will take around three weeks to germinate and even after that they'll grow slowly. That gives you enough time to fit in a few rows of radishes or spinach. Before the parsnips bulk up and overtake the bed, the fast-growing crop will have been harvested.

Carrots can be harvested several times, gradually increasing the distance between individual plants in a row

Prolonged harvesting

Even though we would like our kitchen garden to function like the fairy tale wishing-table and provide a never-ending supply of meals, the fact is that since we're mostly dealing with annual vegetables, we'll have to start from scratch every year. Nevertheless, if we employ a few smart harvesting techniques, we can often substantially prolong the harvest period and increase the yield. Some vegetables will regrow after harvesting and some leafy plants can be cut repeatedly. In other cases you can eat more parts of the plants than those for which they are normally grown. An added bonus of some of these methods is that since you're not always harvesting the whole plant at once, you're not constantly creating empty spots in your beds and the garden keeps looking pretty and abundant most of the season.

HARVEST-THINNING

Many seeds are so tiny that it is difficult to direct-sow them at the correct spacing and timely thinning is usually necessary to achieve strong and healthy plants. It seems a pity to throw away so much potential harvest, but luckily, in many cases the thinnings can be eaten too. I like to spread the thinning over the course of several weeks (or even months), gradually increasing the distance between individual plants in a row. This way you can harvest the vegetables at different stages of growth, each stage having its own charm and different possibilities in the kitchen.

Take for example beetroot: the seeds are fairly large and therefore easier to handle than many others. However, every seed is in fact a cluster of seeds and will therefore usually produce multiple plants. As soon as the seedlings are a couple of centimetres tall, you can thin them to several centimetres spacing. The young tender leaves are delicious raw, in a mixed salad or added to a sandwich. When you thin a little later, the leaves will be larger and suited to sautéing or stirring into a potato mash (something the Dutch will do with just about any vegetable). In the next round of thinning,

February
April
August

July
October
November

After cutting, the mustard greens are left to regrow

Radish seed pods are a nice addition to salads

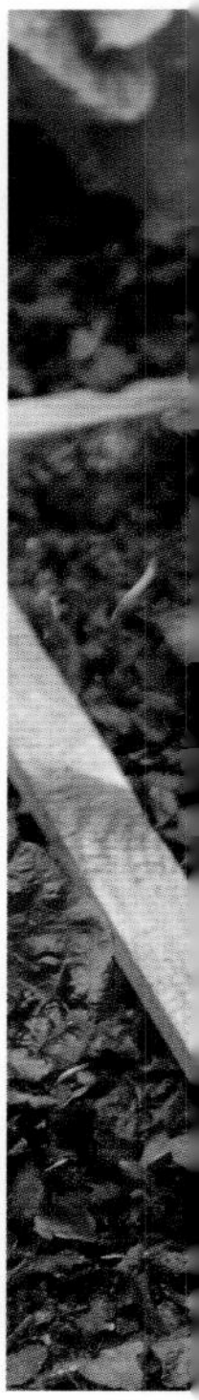

you'll be harvesting table-tennis-ball-sized roots, a gourmet mini-vegetable. And so you will proceed until the last roots left in the soil have enough space to grow into large balls for storage.

Other examples you can harvest in a similar manner are turnips and carrots. Be careful with the vegetables from the nightshade family though since their leaves are not really suited to eating.

CUT-AND-COME-AGAIN

For cut-and-come-again, harvesting seeds are sown close together and seedlings are not thinned. As soon as the plants are about 10cm (4in) tall (this can be as soon as four weeks from sowing), they are cut at about 2-2.5cm (1in) above the ground. After cutting, you let them regrow and then harvest again, up to three, or even four times. The leaves you pick are super tender and contain up to twice as many vitamins as full-grown salad plants. Because the plants are harvested relatively fast, cut-and-come-again salads are very useful as a catch crop before or after a main crop, as well as for intercropping anywhere where there's an empty space in the garden. For example in spring before heat-loving crops such as tomatoes or squashes can be planted out, or at the end of summer after another crop has finished.

This method is only suitable for leafy vegetables, but there is more than lettuce, spinach and rocket. Many different plants from the cabbage family can be grown and harvested this way, for example, different varieties of mustard greens, but also Oriental brassicas such as pak choi or tatsoi. I like to create colourful patterns in the garden by alternating rows of leaves in varying shades of purple and green.

ROOT TO LEAF

In many cases you can eat more of the plant than you might think and this too is a way to

Repeatedly harvesting the outer leaves of lettuce spreads the harvest over a long time

vary, increase and prolong your harvest. For example, during a warm spring, your radishes might bolt before they produce any roots to speak of. Do not pull them out immediately, but wait a little until they start forming green seed pods. These are delightfully crunchy and have the same radish flavour – they make a great addition to salads. Rocket that has bolted will produce masses of edible white flowers with a nice peppery flavour. The yellow or white flowers of all the plants from the cabbage family are edible too and the flowering stems can be dipped in a batter and fried as tempura. In squashes, only the female flowers will grow into fruits (you can recognise them by the embryonic fruit at their base). The male flowers with long slender stems are necessary for pollination but will not produce fruits. You can harvest them and use them as the Italians do: fill the blossom with cheese, dip in batter and fry. I also like adding the sunny yellow flowers to risottos or frittatas. Don't forget that even the leaves of winter squashes are edible – quickly sautéed they make a nice side dish.

Another part of a vegetable that often ends up on the compost heap but actually makes pretty good eating is the top of a Brussels sprout plant. The leaves on top make a loose cabbage head that can be cut off and eaten. Cutting off the top of the plant will also stimulate an even ripening of the tiny sprouts so that they can be harvested all at once.

Bolted lettuce has a tall thick stem – the leaves at this point are usually too bitter and only good for a stir fry, but the stem can be cut and peeled to reveal the crunchy inside that is nice to eat raw.

LEAF-BY-LEAF

In commercial gardens, vegetables are often harvested whole in order to make the harvesting process more efficient. But for a home gardener it makes more sense to keep harvesting from the same plants over a long period of time. So instead of cutting a whole kale plant at once, it is better to just pick the largest leaves from several plants at a time. The kale plants will keep growing and in the end will produce a higher overall yield, spread over a longer period of time.

Chard and lettuce too can be harvested in this fashion by always only picking the outer leaves. Especially with lettuce, this is a handy way to prolong the lifespan of the plants – because they need a certain root to leaf ratio in order to flower, continuous harvesting prevents them from bolting too soon. This harvesting method is best suited to loose-leaf types of lettuces such as 'Lollo Rossa', 'Lollo Bionda', oakleaf lettuce, and the different varieties of romaine and Batavian lettuces. It is less suitable for the classic butterheads that form a tight head.

LETTING REGROW

Many vegetables will regrow if you cut them at a young stage, but some will even do it if they have been harvested at full size. If, after harvesting a head of red cabbage or a cauliflower, you leave the stem behind, it will usually sprout again and form up to four miniature cabbages. You can stimulate the plant to do so by cutting a deep cross in the stub that is left behind after harvesting. To prevent rotting, bend a leaf to cover the stub. Broccoli too will keep producing numerous tiny rosettes after the central one has been harvested. As long as you keep picking and preventing the plant from forming seed, you can keep on harvesting.

Certain varieties of lettuce (for example 'Marvel of Four Seasons') will sometimes even form a secondary head after the first one has been harvested, but most will just produce loose leaves. These are of course also perfectly edible. A nice side-effect of this treatment is that once the large leaves have been cut off, the leftover plants are much less susceptible to frost. Take, for example, radicchio or sugar loaf chicory: when you harvest the heart in fall, the rest of the plant can survive winter pretty easily and as soon as the temperatures start rising in spring, it will usually sprout again. The loose leaves are a very welcome addition to salads in early spring when there is precious little to pick in the garden.

After cutting the main head, miniature cauliflowers will sprout

Both summer and winter squash flowers can be used for this recipe – I pick whatever is available and usually use a mix of both. This recipe is especially suited for using the male squash flowers, which won't produce fruits anyway.

Squash blossom frittata

8 summer or winter squash blossoms
1 spring onion
A small bunch of parsley
8 eggs
Salt, pepper
1 tbsp olive oil
1 ball of mozzarella cheese, cut into thick slices

Preheat oven to 190°C (375°F).

Roughly chop four of the flowers, finely slice the onion (both white and green part) and chop the parsley.

In a medium bowl, whisk the eggs until frothy and mix in the chopped flowers, parsley and onion. Season to taste with salt and pepper.

Heat the olive oil in an ovenproof skillet over medium heat until fairly hot. Pour in the beaten eggs and cook for one minute. Put the skillet in the preheated oven and bake until just set, about 10 minutes. Top with mozzarella and the four remaining squash blossoms. Return to the oven and bake further until the cheese is melted and the frittata is set, about five minutes more.

CHAPTER 6

Extending the Seasons

While it is not difficult to fill our harvest basket with a variety of produce from the garden during the summer months, it becomes a lot harder in winter and early spring. To enjoy lots of variety during the colder months too, it can be necessary to employ a few tools. I am not talking about growing tomatoes in a heated greenhouse year round, which in our climate would require an enormous amount of energy and would only yield rather tasteless fruits. I prefer to seek simple low-input solutions that are within everyone's reach and only make use of passive warming.

During most of our winters, we are able to keep harvesting hardy vegetables such as leeks, kale and parsnips outside. This limited assortment can be supplemented with many more crops, provided we give them some protection from the elements. Obviously, these crops too need to be at least moderately hardy and able to handle a few degrees of frost.

Row covers

A very simple way to extend the season a little on both ends is to cover a bed with some kind of row cover, fleece or film. Under the cover, both the soil and the air will warm up faster so that we can start sowing or transplanting earlier. But even more important than the protection against cold is the protection the cover provides against wind. Creating a more hospitable microclimate will not only bring the harvest a few weeks forward, but will also increase the overall yield and its quality.

A big advantage of row covers is that they can easily be moved around the garden throughout the season to protect different crops. Apart from horticultural fleece, I also have two pieces of heavy-duty insect netting which are long and wide enough to cover our beds. Here's an example of how I use them during the season:

In March, I use one to cover a bed in which I sow radishes, leaf mustard and lettuce. The second one is used to cover a bed into which I transplant pre-sown broad bean plants. In April I move one net to a bed with early potatoes to protect them from possible night frosts. The other is moved to a bed in which I plant early sowings of brassicas such as kohlrabi and broccoli – it provides a little extra warmth but also protects the crop against insects. In May, the netting can be used to protect frost-sensitive crops such as tomatoes or bush beans, so that they can be planted out a little earlier without halting their growth. Later, in July and August, the netting will protect Oriental brassicas such as pak choi, tatsoi and Chinese cabbages from insects. In fall, I put the netting over late sowings of spinach and other moderately hardy leaf vegetables, such as rocket, to extend their harvest.

Horticultural fleece

Fleece is made out of unwoven polypropylene and permeates both air and water. It allows about 70% of light to pass through (depending on thickness) and will protect plants against sunburn. Not unimportant is also the protection it provides from drying winds. Fleece is very light, which means it can be placed directly on top of plants.

It is available in three different thicknesses and, of course, the thicker the material, the more protection against frost it will provide. Fleece of 17g/m^2 will protect plants up to about -2 to -3°C (28-26°F), fleece of 30g/m^2 will protect up to about -5 to -6°C frost (23-21°F). When fleece freezes, it forms an insulation layer (the so-called 'igloo-effect'). Fleece will also protect plants against insects, as long as there are no holes or openings on the sides. Because this material 'breathes', overheating is not an issue and that means it can also be used to protect crops against pests during the summer months. For example, I like to use fleece to cover carrots – in the beginning it provides a little extra warmth for the emerging seedlings; later it offers protection against carrot fly. Horticultural fleece is available in a variety of widths, typically from 110-200cm (3ft7in-6ft6in), and in different lengths. The material is more expensive than plastic film but still relatively cheap. Unfortunately it tears quite easily, even when handled with care, and therefore usually does not last very long.

Plastic film

Transparent plastic film is made out of polyethylene and available in varying thicknesses. Before buying, always check whether the film is UV-resistant. Light plastic film can be laid on top of plants; the heavier kind (usually sold as 'greenhouse film') is best stretched over plastic or metal hoops to create a low tunnel. Underneath the film, soil will warm up quickly, but thin film does not offer much protection against frost. On warm days, temperature can rise rapidly, possibly damaging the plants underneath and the limited airflow also increases chances of fungal disease. It is therefore very important to vent regularly by lifting the film on one side, and to remove the film altogether as soon as the weather warms up. This means that plastic film has to be removed much earlier than materials such as fleece, which breathe more.

There's also perforated film on the market, where about 5% of the surface of the film is holes. This improves air circulation but also means the film offers no protection against insects. You can make perforated film yourself by burning 1cm wide holes into the film about 4-5cm (1½-2in) apart. This works out to about 200 holes per square metre. By burning the holes with a poker, instead of cutting, the edges are sealed and the film will not tear.

Insect netting

As the name suggests, insect netting is mainly meant to protect plants against insect damage. However, the heavy-duty kind of netting especially will also provide plants with some extra warmth. Years ago I invested in two pieces of very sturdy netting with a mesh size of 0.27 x 0.77mm made of UV-resistant polyethylene, weighing 123g/m^2. The extremely small mesh size means it offers protection against just about any insect, even the tiny ones like white fly. Since it also creates a warm sheltered microclimate, it can be used to protect early plantings in spring as well as plantings at the end of the season. Because this insect netting is heavier than both fleece and light film, it is better not to lay it directly on top of the crops. Stretched over PVC or metal hoops, it will even protect the crop against hail. The netting was much more expensive than the other materials (25 Euro for 2 x 5m/6.5x 16.5ft), but it has definitely proven to be much more durable. I have been using it for six years now and it's still in perfect condition.

Insect netting is too heavy to lay directly on the crops

TIPS FOR USING ROW COVERS

1. Try to make sure the soil is weed free to begin with because under the shelter of a row cover, weeds too will grow rapidly. You can cover the bed prior to sowing to warm up the soil and to simultaneously stimulate weed seeds to germinate. You can then hoe off the weeds and proceed to sow or plant your crop.
2. If you're laying the row cover directly on top of your plants, do not stretch it too tightly so that there's room for the plants to grow. However, it shouldn't be too loose either, because then there is more chance it will get damaged by strong winds.
3. The edges of a row cover need to be secured well. You can dig them in or secure them with metal pegs (tent pegs can be used). I prefer to weigh the edges down with bricks because these are easier to remove when I want to lift the cover for ventilation, watering or harvesting. Another good option is bags filled with sand. In fact, these might be preferable when you're using fleece since they will not cause it to tear as quickly as bricks might.
4. If you're sowing under a row cover that is lying directly on the ground, it is a good idea to sow in slightly sunken drills. This way the young plants can get established before they have to push against the row cover.
5. You can spread your harvest by only covering a portion of your crop. For example, if you sow lettuce and only cover half of it with a row cover, the plants under the cover will mature faster. This way you can prevent excess even if you're just sowing once.

Cold frame

From *Naturalis Historia* by Pliny the Elder, we know that the Romans already made use of beds made of basketwork and covered with sheets of mica, in order to supply their emperor Tiberius with his favourite vegetable, cucumbers, all the year round. Many centuries later, the kitchen gardens of large estates often contained 'frameyards' with whole rows of cold frames, with sides made of bricks and covered with specially made 'lights'. Sometimes these were even heated from underneath with hot water pipes so that they could provide out of season crops of strawberries, lettuces, potatoes and cut flowers. But even an unheated cold frame is remarkably effective and can considerably broaden the possibilities of what you grow and when you harvest it – there's definitely a place for one in a contemporary garden too!

Before we were able to buy our current plot, we had been renting an allotment garden and were never sure how long we could keep it. So no matter how much I wanted a greenhouse, we decided against investing in such a permanent structure. Instead, we opted for a simple cold frame and used it intensively.

You can of course buy a cold frame and there are countless models on the market, varying in size, durability and price. But if you have a saw, a screwdriver, a few boards and an old windowpane, you can easily make one yourself.

When our friends replaced their old bedroom windows with double glazed ones, we asked whether we could have the old

In summer, the cold frame is used to grow melons

windowpanes to use for a cold frame. The panes were 123 x 77cm (48 x 30in) and we had two of them so that determined the size of our cold frame – 154 x 123cm (60 x 48in). Cold frames can be quite shallow (e.g. 18cm/7in high at the front and 23cm/9in at the back) and that is fine for growing salads, but because we wanted to use the frame year round and for taller crops as well, we decided to make it quite a bit deeper: 25cm/10in high at the front and 50cm/20in at the back. We bought a couple of Douglas pine boards at a local sawmill (the same ones we use for our raised beds on account of the wood's natural resistance to rot). We cut the boards to size, cutting one of the shorter pieces on a diagonal to create the slope, and screwed them together at the corners. The two window panes were then hinged to the back of the frame, so that they could be easily propped up for ventilation.

When positioning the frame in the garden, keep in mind that the low side has to face south in order to receive maximum sunlight and make optimum use of passive solar heating. Because we used our frame to grow mostly the same crops every year and we wanted to avoid disease build-up (a lot of the winter salads belong to the Brassica family and are prone to clubroot on our sandy soil), we decided to rotate the frame over three different spots at the back of the garden. We used reclaimed tiles for paths and created three small beds of 150 x 120cm/5ft1in x 4ft. This way the frame could be moved every spring and would only return to the same spot every three years. Because the frame was placed on the tiles instead of directly on the soil, the wood was better protected against rot too.

Sowing hardy greens in September

HERE'S HOW WE USED OUR COLD FRAME DURING THE YEAR:

Spring

The new season for our cold frame officially started in May when it was moved to a new location. Prior to the move, we added a layer of well-rotted manure or compost to the soil to provide nutrients for the heavy feeders that would be grown there. Many crops can be grown in a cold frame but to make the best use of the space we chose those that would benefit from the extra heat the most. In the second half of April I started two melon plants indoors – one per windowpane. Against the back of the frame, we planted a few basil plants and one or two chilli peppers. We mulched the soil with a thick layer of straw to limit evaporation and the need for watering. When the melon fruits started forming, they would rest on a bed of straw, which would protect them from rotting. The frame was ventilated every time we visited the allotment and when it got warmer, we left one pane permanently propped up. Ideally it would have been left open during the day and closed at night but since we did not live that close to the garden, this was not possible.

The fruits of melon 'Minnesota Midget' are small but deliciously sweet

Summer

When hot temperatures set in, we took the panes off completely and let the melons trail out of the frame. When we came back from vacation towards the end of August, there would usually already be a few fruits waiting to be harvested. Even just two plants gave us a reasonable harvest of delicious fruits. Melons fresh from the garden are a rare treat for gardeners in our climate! In a good summer we could get up to six fruits per plant, but they were not big as the cultivars suited to our climate are usually small-fruited. Over the years, I had tried several different varieties: 'Minnesota Midget', 'Petit Gris de Rennes', 'Collective Farm Woman' and 'Golden Midget' (a mini water melon). Out of these, 'Petit Gris de Rennes' was the best tasting and 'Minnesota Midget' the most reliable. As soon as the melons finished fruiting, we took the plants out and raked away the straw, which we either added to the compost heap or reused as mulch elsewhere in the garden.

Autumn

Around mid-September, I sowed different hardy salad plants in 10cm (4in) wide strips: rocket, mibuna, mizuna and other kinds of mustards, chrysanthemum greens shungiku, leaf chicory 'Zuccherina di Trieste', winter purslane, land cress, buckhorn plantain, pak choi and corn salad. In September the soil is still warm and the seeds germinated quickly. If the seedlings turned out to be too close together, a little thinning was needed, but of course all the thinnings were eaten. Approximately five weeks after sowing, the plants could be cut for the first time, about 2cm (1in) above the ground, after which they were left to regrow. The speed with which they'd regrow, as well as the number of cuts we could expect, differed per variety. Some of these leafy vegetables

In winter the cold frame grows different kinds of hardy salad greens

(especially corn salad, winter purslane, and plantain) are hardy enough to survive our winters without any protection, but the extra heat provided by the cold frame meant they would regrow faster and provide more pickings. At the end of October or the beginning of November, when the temperature dropped, we would put the panes back on. Further maintenance was minimal: the plants do not need watering during winter and there are few pests around.

Winter

The salads from the cold frame, in combination with the smaller leaves of kale and chicories that overwinter outside, provided us with a weekly salad, except maybe during the darkest weeks of the year around Christmas when plant growth stops due to low light levels.

The promise of a fresh salad had the power to lure us to the allotment even in the middle of winter when we otherwise probably wouldn't go. While we were there, we would usually also tackle a few small jobs. A bit of weeding here and mulching there when we came to pick our salad meant that we stayed on top of things and in spring the garden was ready for the next season.

Spring

As soon as it got warmer, the plants in the cold frame started running to seed. The leaves that were still palatable were harvested; the rest was pulled out and added to the compost heap. Any empty spaces were then used for sowing extra early crops like radishes, carrots and lettuce. In May the frame was moved to a new location and the cycle started again ...

CHAPTER 7

Keeping the Garden in Good Health

Crop rotation

Crop rotation is a millennia old practice which requires you to move crops around your garden in such a way that vegetables belonging to the same botanical family do not grow in the same spot year after year. Usually it is recommended to let at least three or four years pass before the planting of related crops is repeated and the longer the better.

If you garden in permanent (raised) beds, crop rotation is relatively easy to plan and to practise. There are many good reasons to implement it: different crops extract different nutrients from the soil and by alternating the crops you grow in a given bed, you prevent the soil from being depleted. Related crops are often susceptible to the same pests and diseases and by moving them around you can prevent the build-up of problems. Crop rotation also makes it possible for us to make use of the many subtle ways in which plants can benefit each other. For example, all plants from the legume family, such as broad beans and peas, are capable of fixing nitrogen in tiny nodules on their roots. If, after harvesting the crop, you leave the roots in the soil, and you follow with a nitrogen-hungry crop such as cabbages or leeks, that second crop will grow noticeably better. I once tested this by planting Brussels sprouts in a bed where broad beans were grown in the first half of the season, but only on half the area – there was a big difference in growth between the sprouts that grew where the beans had been and those in the other half of the bed. Another example of a beneficial follow-up is growing brassicas after plants from the onion family. Onions have fungicidal properties and can help to prevent fungal disease in the following crop; in the case of cabbage, clubroot could be a problem.

However, planning crop rotation gets significantly more complicated when, as I recommended in the previous chapter, you grow more than one crop per season in each bed. If possible, try not to follow early peas with bush beans or mustard greens with pak choi. That being said, it is less important to take into account crops that spend a relatively short time in the ground (such as radishes and spinach) than crops that occupy the bed for many months. Moreover, not all crops are equally sensitive to disease. If your soil is healthy, you can probably get away with bending the rules a bit.

Raised beds make crop rotation easy to implement

Companion planting

Many gardening books advise you to combine two different crops within a bed in order to benefit from their mutually positive influence. In many cases, these combinations (or 'good neighbours') are based on the simple fact that a strong scent of one of the crops will mask the scent of the other and thus confuse the pests a crop is prone to. This is also the reasoning behind one of the best known combinations: onions and carrots. The scent of onions keeps carrot fly at bay, while the scent of carrots is supposed to protect onions from onion fly. Unfortunately, when this combo was tested, it was only found to be effective against carrot fly when four times as many onions as carrots were grown and this is probably not a ratio most gardeners need.

In other cases, the reason behind a good or bad combination is less clear and the recommendations of different authors can be quite contradictory. What one gardener perceives as a good combination, another one would not recommend. Presumably, the difference in their experience can be accounted for by the fact that there are many more factors at play than what two crops are growing next to each other: In what soil are they growing? How much manure, water and attention do they get from the gardener? In short, what works in one garden will not necessarily work in another but in general, the more variety, the fewer problems you're likely to encounter.

Polyculture

Which brings us to an even more radical approach to vegetable growing: polycultures. Instead of assigning each crop a separate bed or combining just two, we can also merrily sow and plant everything together in a proper polyculture. When we look to nature for guidance, we'll quickly discover that it deals neither in monocultures nor simple planting combinations. We'll likely find complex communities wherein plants support each other in countless ways in order to create a healthy, flexible and resilient whole. Since one of the most important principles of permaculture gardening is diversity, polycultures are often practised on permaculture plots.

It's more difficult to create functional plant communities in the kitchen garden where most of the crops are annual plants than it is in an edible forest garden full of perennials, but even here we can benefit from some of the advantages of polycultures. It can take a little courage to let go of the neat rows, but mixing different kinds of plants together can have many benefits. Because different plants need different nutrients and have varying root systems, they can often coexist quite happily and grow close together without competing. This means we can obtain a larger yield from a given space than if we are just growing one crop. Many plants have other interesting properties beside their edibility, which can come in handy in a polyculture. As I mentioned before, plants from the onion family have antifungal properties. Plants from the carrot family such as dill attract beneficial insects (e.g. hoverflies), which in turn keep aphids in check. But no matter what plants exactly you combine, diversity in itself is an insurance policy against major pests and disease problems.

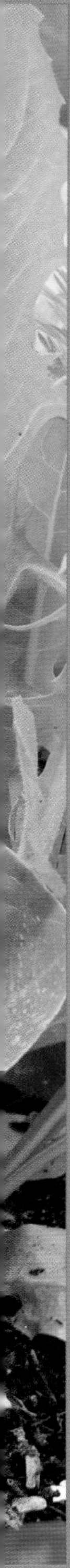

Plant families

THE CABBAGE FAMILY (Brassicaceae)

Kale, cauliflower, broccoli, Chinese cabbage, kohlrabi, turnip, mustard greens, mibuna, mizuna, pak choi, tatsoi, cabbages, radish, rocket, Brussels sprouts, collards, sea kale

THE SUNFLOWER FAMILY (Asteraceae)

Lettuces, chicories, Belgian endive, artichokes, Jerusalem artichokes, cardoon, salsify, tarragon

THE ONION FAMILY (Alliaceae)

Onions, leek, garlic, shallots, spring onions, chives, garlic chives, Welsh onion, nodding onions, Egyptian onions

THE CUCUMBER FAMILY (Cucurbitaceae)

Cucumbers, melons, summer squash, winter squash

THE LEGUME FAMILY (Leguminosae or Fabaceae)

Peas, sugar snap peas, snow peas, broad beans, green beans, shell beans, runner beans, asparagus peas, edamame beans, lupin

THE BEET FAMILY (Chenopodiaceae)

Beetroot, chard, spinach, orache, quinoa, Good King Henry

THE NIGHTSHADE FAMILY (Solanaceae)

Potatoes, tomatoes, peppers, aubergines, tomatillos

THE CARROT (Apiaceae or Umbelliferae)

Carrots, celery, celeriac, fennel, parsnips, Hamburg parsley, dill, chervil, parsley, coriander, lovage

THE GRAIN FAMILY (Poaceae)

Corn, wheat, rye, oat, millet

THE KNOTWEED FAMILY (Polygonaceae)

Rhubarb, sorrel, buckwheat

THE PURSLANE FAMILY (Portulacaceae)

Winter purslane (claytonia), summer purslane

THE VALERIAN FAMILY (Valerianaceae)

Corn salad (mâche)

THE ASPARAGUS FAMILY (Asparagaceae)

Asparagus

THE MINT FAMILY (Lamiaceae or Labiatae)

Basil, mint, oregano, marjoram, thyme, anise hyssop, sage, rosemary

THE MORNING GLORY FAMILY (Convolvulaceae)

Sweet potatoes

THE ROSE FAMILY (Rosaceae)

Strawberries, raspberries, blueberries, blackberries

CHAPTER 8

Seeds for Your Garden

Seed saving

Since the majority of the plants grown in the kitchen garden are either annuals or biennials, new seeds are needed every year. Many gardeners, especially those striving for self-sufficiency, will probably quickly start asking themselves whether seed saving would be a good idea. Besides saving money and providing a sense of independence, seed saving has other potential benefits. Seeds that you buy will usually have been grown under different circumstances, in different soil and in a slightly different climate. By saving seed from plants that have grown in your garden, you can over time develop strains that are well adapted to the specific circumstances of your surroundings. You can even adapt a certain variety to your preferences, by saving seed from plants that display more of the characteristics that you are after. But even though any vegetable plant will eventually set seed if you let it flower, it is not an entirely simple matter to keep a variety true to type and to save good quality seed that will reliably germinate. Here are a few things to keep in mind if you want to try your hand at seed saving:

1. Hybrid or open-pollinated?

Hybrid seeds are marked as F1 and are the first generation offspring resulting from a cross between two different varieties. Because of this they often display extra vigour or other desirable qualities such as resistance to certain diseases. Unfortunately, unlike in old, heirloom varieties, these characteristics have not been stabilised through a long-term selection process. Were you to save seeds from these plants, the next generation would not be identical to the mother plants but would display a varied mix of characteristics inherited from its grandparents. Therefore it is best only to save seeds from open-pollinated, not hybrid varieties.

2. Annual or biennial?

Annual vegetables will produce seeds in their first year, biennial only in their second. Carrots for example are a biennial plant and that means that for seed saving you have to harvest them in fall, select a number of good roots and overwinter them in a frost-free environment. In spring, you can plant them in the garden again and only then will they flower and produce seeds. If you are planning to save seed from biennial vegetables, you have to keep in mind that they will occupy space in the garden much longer than when you just grow them to eat. Apart from carrots, other biennials include parsnips, leeks, onions, salsify, beetroot, chard, celery, celeriac and all kinds of cabbages.

3. Self-pollinating or cross-pollinating?

In self-pollinating vegetables, the flowers contain both female and male organs and are thus able to pollinate themselves. If the flower is quite closed, there is also a smaller chance of

it being pollinated by insects that could bring in pollen from another plant and with it a different set of genes. This is why self-pollinating vegetables will generally come true from seed. The majority of vegetables however are not self-pollinating and that means that if there is another, related plant flowering in the vicinity at the same time, cross-pollination might occur. Cross-pollination will result in changes in the genetic makeup of the plants and you never know what you'll get if you sow the seeds. For example, the aforementioned carrot could be pollinated not only by other carrot varieties, but also by the widely spread wild carrot and its varieties often grown as cut flowers. Cross-pollination can occur over long distances, often hundreds of metres. If your garden is relatively isolated and you only allow one variety to flower at a time, you can probably prevent cross-pollination. However, if your garden is surrounded by other gardens, it might be a lot more difficult and you might need to create physical barriers for insects, such as cages enclosed in insect netting.

4. How long will seeds keep?

How long seeds remain viable depends largely on the specific kind of vegetable. Tomato seeds for example will often keep for more than five years, while carrot seeds will only last a year or two. This means that you'd only need to save tomato seeds once every five years, but you'd need to do it every year for carrots. The temperature at which seeds are stored is also very important – you can double the lifespan of seeds by storing them in air-tight containers in the fridge instead of at room temperature. Another important factor is whether the seeds are allowed to ripen fully on the plant. The longer they stay on the plant, the more reserves they can build up and the longer they will last in storage.

Considering all of the above, you could quickly come to the conclusion that saving seeds from certain vegetables would be too complicated or even unattainable. But do not give up on seed saving altogether – it can be a fun and satisfying thing to do. Below you will find information on the easiest vegetables to start with. In order to keep a reasonably wide genetic basis and to prevent inbreeding, it is wise to save seeds from at least six (or more) plants at a time. In the case of fruiting vegetables, it is also a good idea to save seeds from several fruits from each plant, both some that ripened early and some that ripened later in the season. And of course, only ever harvest seeds from healthy plants – some diseases can be transmitted through seed! Store your seeds dry and cool and always label them including the year when the seed was harvested.

Borlotti beans drying on the plant

EASY VEGETABLES TO START WITH

Beans and peas

Saving seed from all kinds of beans (broad beans, bush beans, climbing beans, edamame) and peas (shelling peas, sugar snaps, snow peas) is easy since the seeds are exactly the part of the plant that we consume and the only thing required to save seeds is to leave the pods on the plant until they are dry and can be stored. Apart from the runner bean (*Phaseolus coccineus*) and broad bean (*Vicia faba*), peas and beans are mostly self-pollinating and will therefore usually come true from seed. The different varieties of runner beans and broad beans will cross-pollinate, but if you only grow one variety, you can save the seeds too. Possible problems are the broad bean weevil *Bruchus rufimanus* and the pea moth *Cydia nigricana*, which lay eggs in the developing seeds and will come out later after the seeds have been stored. Putting the seeds in the freezer for two or three weeks will kill the larvae. Seeds of beans and peas remain viable for about 3-4 years.

Tomatoes, peppers and aubergines

Most tomatoes are self-pollinating, but in peppers and aubergines cross-pollination can occur. In tomatoes it is often some old beefsteak varieties or those genetically close to the wild tomato that might cross-pollinate, but modern varieties usually won't. You can prevent cross-pollination by only growing one variety (for example, I usually stick to growing just one hot pepper), or if space allows, growing different varieties far apart (for aubergine the recommended distance is 25 metres). For tomato varieties that might cross-pollinate you can also enclose a truss in a piece of insect

netting. To save seeds from peppers, you just extract the seeds from over-ripe fruits and dry them. Tomato seeds have a protective layer that prevents the seeds from sprouting inside the moist environment of a fruit. To remove the layer, extract the seeds from a fruit with a spoon and put them in a glass jar with a little water. Leave the jar in a warm spot until a layer of mould appears. Then rinse the seeds well and let them dry. The seeds of the vegetables above remain viable for about 4-5 years (longer for tomatoes and aubergines).

Lettuce and endive

Both are self-pollinating and will therefore usually come true from seed, especially if you keep different varieties separated by at least three metres. Do not save the seed of plants that run to seed early since you'd be selecting for premature bolting and that is definitely

Left: Most tomato varieties are self-pollinating

Right: Flowering lettuce

not a desirable trait in either lettuce or endive. When the seeds of lettuce are ripe, they will resemble dandelion with a 'fluff' on top. The seeds tend to ripen unevenly, so it is a good idea to pick them every few days. Alternatively, pick the flowering stalk when about half the seeds are ripe and put it in a paper bag or a bucket where they can further ripen and dry. Since one lettuce plant produces a copious amount of seeds, even half of it will be plenty. For endive it is best to wait until about ⅔ of the seeds are ripe before you pick the stalk. Lettuce seed keeps for about 3-4 years, endive usually a little longer.

Cucumber, melons and summer and winter squash

The seeds of these fruiting vegetables are some of the largest and easiest to extract. However, they are pollinated by insects and can cross with other plants from the same botanical group over a large distance. All cucumbers and gherkins (*Cucumis sativus*) can cross with each other, but if you only grow one variety in a greenhouse, you might get away with saving seed from it. The same goes for melons. Squashes cross readily and the only way to make sure you keep a variety true to type, is to hand pollinate. For this, you need to select a male and a female flower (the female flower has an embryo fruit right under the blossom) that are just about to open and tie the ends of the petals together with a string or a rubber band to prevent insects from entering. The next day, take the male flower and transfer the pollen from it onto the stigma at the centre of the female flower. Then carefully close the flower again and tie a piece of wool loosely around the stem to mark the developing fruit. After harvesting, let the fruit ripen for an additional month or so before extracting the seeds. The seeds keep for about 5-6 years.

Self-sowing vegetables

Several years ago, when the lease of our first allotment expired, we had to move to another plot. When we went back in spring two years later to see how our ex-garden had fared, we discovered that unlike on the neighbouring plots that were completely overgrown with weeds, there were still plenty of edible plants to pick on ours: several varieties of mustard greens, colourful orache and mild-tasting winter purslane. Because we had allowed different vegetables to self-seed in the previous years, I could still pick a varied spring salad from a plot that had not been gardened for almost two years.

Letting vegetables self-seed is even easier than saving seeds to sow yourself and it provides many of the same benefits. You don't need to keep buying seeds and the plants will adapt somewhat to your soil and climate. Many vegetables, such as kales or orache, have beautiful flowers. Those flowers attract beneficial insects into the garden and are a source of nectar for pollinators. On top of that, self-sowers have a few additional advantages. For one, you do not need to worry about when exactly is the best time to sow. When the circumstances are right, the seeds will automatically sprout. Furthermore, the enormous amount of seed most plants produce is in itself an insurance against failure. Just one plant will often produce the equivalent of many seed packets. Seeds can be lost because they'll rot or be eaten by critters, but there will still be enough to ensure the emergence of the next generation.

Even though virtually any vegetable can be left to self-seed, when cross-pollination occurs, the offspring will not always display the same qualities as the mother plant. In our cool climate, it is also not practical to let tender vegetables such as peppers or aubergines self-seed. They need high temperatures to germinate and by the time these occur in the garden, it is too late for the plants to grow into maturity and produce fruits in our short season. Another issue is the transmission of disease – spontaneously emerging tomatoes can harbour blight and vegetables from the cabbage family (Brassicaceae) could play host to club root. Not all vegetables are therefore suitable for this laissez-faire approach and even the suitable ones will require a bit of management. In my experience, the most reliable self-sowers are often leafy vegetables. In other types of vegetables, for example those grown for their swollen roots like beets or turnips, the self-sown offspring will often bolt before forming any edible root.

As in all vegetables, if you'd always only allowed one plant to form seeds, this could over time lead to inbreeding. It will not happen as quickly in vegetables that are still relatively close to their wild form, as it will in cultivars that are the result of multiple crosses and a long selection process. But to be on the safe side, if space allows, it is always better to allow multiple plants to flower thus keeping the genetic base wider.

SELF-SEEDING EDIBLES IN FIVE STEPS

1. Choose several strong, well-developed plants which you want to self-seed. Preferably, do not harvest from these to prevent depleting their energy.
2. Some edibles form tall flowering stalks – support those with a bamboo cane to prevent them from breaking.
3. When the seeds are ripe, you can either let them fall to the ground where the plant has grown, or cut the stalk and move it to a different part of the garden. You can also just add it to the compost heap, so that the seeds will be distributed throughout the garden through application of compost. (I often do this.)
4. The seedlings of the self-sown plants will likely come up quite close together – if you want them to grow into strong plants, you'll need to thin them. The seedlings of all the plants I mention on the following pages can be eaten. If you'd rather have the plants grow elsewhere, you can, of course, also replant the seedlings in a different location.
5. Again choose strong healthy plants from the following generation and start with step 1.

A patch of self-sown vegetables with orache, mustard greens and land cress

Mustard greens
(Brassica juncea)

If you sow mustard greens in spring and let the plants form seed, they will produce a second generation within the same season. Because of the brassica's susceptibility to clubroot, a bothersome fungal disease that can remain in the soil for years, it is wise to exercise some caution. The different varieties will cross readily, which I personally do not mind since the hybrids are all edible, but if you want to keep a variety true to kind, it's better to only allow one variety to flower at a time.

Curly mallow
(Malva crispa)

The bright green leaves of mallow with its frivolously curled edges remind me of a cancan dancer's skirt. Its taste is mild and the small leaves are a nice addition to salads, while the larger ones can also be cooked. The tiny white flowers and unripe green seeds are edible too. The texture of the leaves is somewhat mucilaginous and reminiscent of okra. The tall plants are very productive and we often pick from them throughout the summer till deep in autumn since they withstand both hot weather and mild frosts.

Garden orache and tree spinach
(Atriplex hortensis and *Chenopodium giganteum)*

Both orache and tree spinach are very successful self-seeders – I've only ever sown them once, many years ago, and since then they've always been present in my garden. The young red, green or bicolour leaves have a slightly salty taste and are nice in salads; later they can be cooked like spinach. I like to prepare red orache as creamed spinach to serve with pasta – its colour turns the dish a shocking shade of pink.

Winter purslane
(Claytonia perfoliata)

The fragile appearance of winter purslane (also called miner's lettuce) belies its hardiness. The mild-tasting leaves are a basic ingredient of our winter salads. Winter purslane will often self-sow so much it will form a dense carpet but since there is enough space available in the winter garden, I do not mind this in the slightest. In spring, the tiny white flowers will appear.

Flowering mustard

Curly mallow

Tree spinach

Parsley
(*Petroselinum crispum*)

Parsley is a biennial, which means it will overwinter and then flower and form seeds in its second year. If your climate is very cold, you might need to offer the plants some protection. The different varieties of parsley (curly and flat leafed) can cross but if you only grow one kind it will likely not be a problem. And even those that are a result of a cross, you can still eat.

Corn salad
(*Valerianella locusta*)

Another very hardy salad plant that is also known under the names lamb's lettuce and mâche. Its hardiness and nutty taste make it our family's favourite winter salad. In my experience it fares better if I let it self-seed than when I sow it intentionally, because I often struggle with the right timing. Better leave the decision to the plant – it knows best!

Perpetual spinach
(*Beta vulgaris* subsp. *vulgaris*)

One of the most useful greens you can grow, this variety of chard has thinner stems than the more colourful cultivars and it is mostly grown for the spinach-like leaves. It is also hardier than other varieties, which is important since as a biennial it will only flower after overwintering. Perpetual spinach will cross with other varieties of chard and also with beetroot, but if you, like me, only allow this one variety to flower, it will come true.

Land cress
(*Barbarea vulgaris*)

If the temperatures are not too low, we often harvest the spicy tasting leaves of land cress throughout the winter months. If your climate is harsher than ours, you could try protecting the plants with a row cover. In spring, the yellow flowers and then the seeds will appear. In my experience, land cress self-seeds reliably but not aggressively.

Other good candidates for self-sowing:

Annual herbs: dill, chervil, chamomile

Edible flowers: nasturtium, calendula, borage, heartsease

Perennial vegetables: asparagus (not the modern all-male hybrid varieties), Good King Henry, sorrel, salad burnet

Winter purslane

Corn salad

Land cress

This salad is the epitome of my garden in spring: the first radishes and green asparagus with a variety of self-sown leaves, everything tossed with a lemony vinaigrette.

Spring garden salad

450g (1lb) green asparagus
3 spring onions
A bunch of radishes
150g (5oz) mix of self-sown salad leaves such as leaf mustard greens, winter purslane, orache and land cress

DRESSING:

1 tbsp white wine vinegar
1 tsp finely grated lemon zest (from an organic lemon)
1 tsp Dijon mustard
4 tbsp cold-pressed olive oil
1 tbsp freshly squeezed lemon juice
Salt, pepper

Trim the tough ends of the asparagus and slice the spears diagonally in pieces of about 3cm (a bit over 1in), leaving the tops intact. Bring water to boil in a medium pan. Add salt and drop in the asparagus pieces. Boil until just tender, about six minutes. Drain and let cool a bit.

Meanwhile, thinly slice the white parts of the onions and mix them with the vinegar and grated zest in the bottom of a large bowl – let them marinate for at least 10 minutes.

Add mustard, olive oil and lemon juice and whisk everything until smooth. Season with salt and pepper. Add the asparagus, thinly sliced radishes and thinly sliced green parts of the onions. Stir to coat the vegetables with the dressing and let stand for a bit for the flavours to marry. Just before serving, gently stir in the leaves.

CHAPTER 9

Tailor-made Kitchen Gardens

In this chapter, I am going to share real life examples of both gardens where crop rotation is practised and those where crops are mixed into different kinds of polycultures. The gardens range from a simple one with just a handful of crops suited for an absolute beginner, to complex polycultures that are not only highly productive but also visually appealing. You can choose which way of gardening suits you best in your current situation and which will make the best use of the space you have available for growing.

A garden to grow up with

Several years ago, when my sister became pregnant, she decided to plant her first ever kitchen garden – without experience or green fingers, but with a deep desire to ensure the best possible diet for her baby once it started eating solid foods. Shortly before our niece was born, my sister and her husband moved into an old house with a large garden in a small, tucked-away village. Space was therefore not an issue, unlike their lack of experience with growing food. To help them get off to a good start, I offered to share my knowledge and practical help setting up the garden.

The most important advice for novice gardeners, 'start small', is even more important in the case of a young family, since it is unlikely that with a baby to care for, there will be lots of time left for gardening. Even though my sister's garden is large, I advised her to start with just three 1.2 x 2.5m (4 x 8ft) beds and expand the garden later, as her child(ren) got older and she gained more experience. In spring, I came to stay for a few days and we got to work. In order to be able to direct-sow vegetables such as carrots already in the first year, we opted for digging the soil and painstakingly removing all roots of perennial weeds by hand. If done properly, this only needs to be done once after which the soil can be left undisturbed. The soil in my sister's garden is heavy clay and the digging was a back-breaking chore – one of the reasons why we normally prefer not to do it! Once the soil was dug and raked over, my children had fun marking the paths by stomping back and forth. Next to the three instant beds in which we could start sowing immediately, an equally large area was covered with cardboard. During the first gardening season, the cardboard would kill the weeds underneath so that in the second year, three new beds could be made on the weed-free soil and the assortment of vegetables grown in the garden could be expanded.

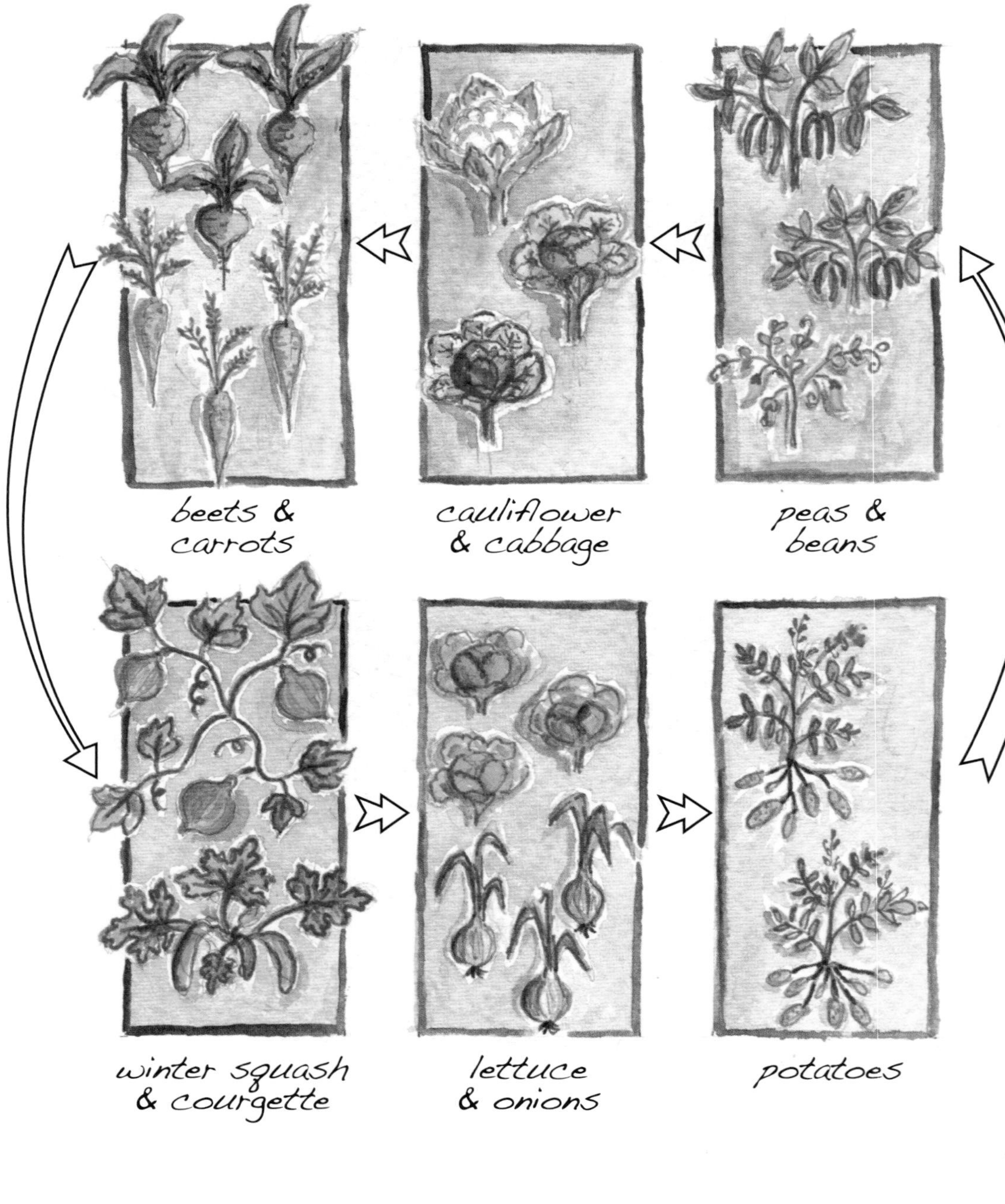
beets &
carrots
cauliflower
& cabbage
peas &
beans
winter squash
& courgette
lettuce
& onions
potatoes

The garden was tailored to growth: the literal growth of the baby, for whom it would be the source of first solid food, and the figurative growth of her mother as a gardener. In time, the garden would grow in size and the planting would get more diverse, while the baby would get a chance to get to know new vegetables. The choice of the first crops was in part determined by their suitability for feeding a young child, while at the same time, I did not want to include crops that are too challenging to grow. I also thought it better to limit the number of vegetables at the beginning in order to keep the garden easy to oversee. Many vegetables, especially leafy greens, are rich in nitrite and therefore less suitable for regular inclusion in a baby's diet. I limited the proportion of these vegetables in the garden but did not exclude them completely as I think variety is important. My own children for example both enjoyed the sweet earthy taste of beetroot, so I wanted to include that too.

Since the number of crops was limited, I decided to introduce more variety by opting for a few seed mixes of different varieties. We sowed a multi-colour mix of beets and carrots, which provided us with white, yellow, red, purple and striped roots. For the cauliflower too, we found a mix of white, green, orange and purple varieties. Not only do these varieties differ in colour, the taste and vitamin content varies too!

Some of the vegetables also lend themselves well to winter storage so that homegrown food can be enjoyed even in the depth of winter. Everything could of course be stored in the freezer, but carrots and beets can also be stored in buckets or boxes between layers of sand in a cellar or a frost-free shed. Winter squash last for months in an unheated bedroom.

The vegetables in this little garden were grouped together according to their needs and the plant families they belong to, in order to make a simple crop rotation possible. Carrots and beets were sown directly, while courgette and winter squash were sown in pots inside, about three weeks before the last expected frost date. Broccoli and cauliflower are also better sown in modules on a sunny windowsill, but if taking care of the seedlings is too much trouble for a young family, they can be sown directly outside.

In order to make an even better use of the beds in the future, some of the crops could be preceded and/or followed with another, fast-growing one.

1st year

Three beds of 1.2 x 2.5m
Bed 1: courgette and winter squash
Bed 2: beets and carrots
Bed 3: cauliflower and broccoli

Next to the beds, an area of 4.5 x 3m was covered with a layer of well-rotted horse manure and large pieces of cardboard. Three winter squash plants were planted through small holes in the cardboard made with a trowel.

2nd year

Six beds of 1.2 x 2.5m
Bed 1: beets and carrots
Bed 2: cauliflower and broccoli
Bed 3: peas and beans
Bed 4: potatoes
Bed 5: lettuce and onions
Bed 6: courgette and winter squash

In the spring of the second year, all beds moved one step forward, so that the bed where squash had been growing would grow carrots and beets. Beds number 2, 4 and 6, where nutrient hungry crops would grow, were amended with a layer of well-rotted manure prior to planting. Bed number 2, where brassicas would be grown, could be amended with lime if the soil is acidic, in order to help prevent club root.

In the coming years, the crops will continue to be rotated and all beds will be manured well at least once every two years. My sister has a horse and a pony and therefore an ample supply of manure. Cow manure or compost would be equally suitable for feeding the soil. The soil in my sister's garden is nutrient-rich clay, but if the soil were sand, the crops in beds number 1, 3 and 5 would also benefit from an annual addition of (preferably homemade) compost.

Winter squash growing through cardboard mulch

Purple cauliflower

I made this salad with beets and carrots from my sister's first year garden when we came to visit in October. While the salad is not suitable for babies, even quite young children usually enjoy raw beetroot in combination with carrots and apples. Needless to say, the salad is full of vitamins and minerals and since beets, carrots and apples can easily be stored, you can prepare it throughout autumn and winter.

Aim for approximately equal parts of beetroot, carrots and apples – below I recorded the quantities I used, but since beetroot, carrots and apples all vary in size, you may need to adjust the quantities.

Beetroot, carrot and apple salad

1 large beetroot
2 medium carrots
2 sweet flavourful apples
¼ cup sunflower seeds

DRESSING:

Juice of 1 small lemon
2 tbsp olive oil
2 tbsp sunflower seed oil

Peel and coarsely grate the beetroot. Peel the carrots and grate them. Halve the apples and remove the core, but do not peel them. Grate the apples as well. Whisk all the ingredients for the dressing together and pour them over the grated vegetables. Toss everything gently. Lightly roast the sunflower seeds and scatter them on top before serving.

Hengelo's first community garden

For many years we used to hold an annual plant fest at the playground in our street where local residents could swap seeds and plants and get advice on organic gardening, beekeeping and backyard poultry raising. But no matter how fun this fest was, it was just one day a year which is why our small team came up with the idea of starting a little community garden that could become a more permanent meeting space for people interested in gardening. Since the garden was to serve an educational purpose too, we wanted it to be in a place frequented by many local residents. The large playground area around our community centre seemed ideal and luckily the board of the community centre was immediately on board. Together we found a suitable spot: A somewhat forlorn corner behind the football cage with grass, lots of weeds and some overgrown bushes. We also obtained a small subsidy from the city to get us started.

In order to inspire as many people as possible to give growing food in their backyards a go, we wanted the garden to be not only productive, but also visually appealing. At the same time, it needed to be easy to care for since it would be managed by a small group of volunteers. Of course, sustainability was important to us as well which meant an absolute ban on pesticides and inorganic fertilisers, reusing all materials on site and composting all garden waste. In April 2012, we got to work. In the course of two mornings, the ground was levelled and covered with large pieces of cardboard to prevent weeds (especially couch grass and ground elder) from regrowing. The community centre collects old paper for recycling so there was enough cardboard for us to use. Directly on top of the cardboard, we placed five square raised beds measuring 1 x 1m made from larch wood which is (just like Douglas pine) an indigenous rot-resistant wood species. We filled the beds with a mix of clean garden soil and compost. The paths were covered with wood chips that we can get for free from the municipality. In order to use the beds as efficiently as possible, we did not sow most of the vegetables directly, but planted pre-sown plants instead. Because we like to involve children from the neighbourhood in the garden as well, it is important that the beds are not too big and that there is enough space around them. Where beds have no edges, it can sometimes be difficult to explain to young children where a bed ends and a path starts but when raised beds are edged with wooden boards, it is not a problem. Raised beds are also easy to care for, especially if they are mulched. After planting, we mulched all the beds with cocoa shells, which gave them a neat appearance and also reduced the necessity of watering and weeding. On 28th May the garden was ready for a celebratory opening during our annual plant fest.

MANY HANDS

The biggest difference between a community garden and a private garden is the number of people involved in caring for it. There are usually enough hands to help with the few bigger jobs such as renewing the wood chip layer on the paths in spring. But aside from that, everyone also brings a piece of themselves, their knowledge and interests and that turns a community garden into a colourful mosaic of the neighbourhood.

My contribution is my knowledge of vegetable growing, but many others have contributed ideas and practical help. Rolf, who enjoys tackling the more physically demanding jobs, also solved the problem of neighbourhood cats making a mess of our freshly sown beds by constructing simple cages from garden mesh. In fall we put them over kale and they double as protection against pigeons. Ryan, who loves flowers, planted a strip of colourful dahlias in a bed edged with tiles we found on site. Ank brought a bird feeder and makes sure it's never empty. Nienke, who had to move the chicken coop in her backyard, brought several barrowloads of good garden soil enriched with chicken manure. Another neighbour brought a pile of old tiles. And then there are the many children who come to play at the playground and who like to follow the changes

The community garden is tended by a small group of volunteers who share the harvests

throughout the seasons. They might not be ready to take on the 'boring' jobs like weeding, but will sometimes spontaneously offer help with hauling water and, of course, they love to snack on sugar snap peas and sun-ripened cherry tomatoes.

Over the years, the garden has gradually expanded – we added eight more half-sized wooden beds and two long narrow ones edged with tiles along two sides of the plot. Wherever possible, we reuse materials we find around the playground or in the neighbourhood. Old tiles on edge are, as I mentioned, a cheap (free) way to edge raised beds and iron poles that were lying around made corners for our compost heaps. We compost not only all the plant waste from the garden, but also vegetable scraps and spent coffee grounds from the kitchen of the community centre. When the adjacent football field is mown, we add the grass clippings to our heap and in fall we gather leaves from the huge beech tree that stands proudly in the middle of the playground. Apart from homemade compost to feed our soil, we also collect well-rotted manure from a pony that grazes in a nearby garden. Sometimes other gardeners will bring us their excess seedlings. We save seed from some vegetables (especially tomatoes and beans) so that we need to buy less.

The community garden has provided us with bountiful harvests that we divide among the volunteers who help to maintain it. When there happens to be an excess of courgettes, we share them with the volunteers from the adjacent community centre. We bring freshly picked bouquets for the community centre's lounge and contribute salads for our street's monthly potluck. But the most important harvest turned out to be improved contacts between neighbourhood residents. On a whim once, I invited our American neighbour to help in the community garden – it gave her the opportunity to meet a few new people, pick up a little Dutch and find inspiration for her own backyard. Some volunteers garden with us for one season and then go on to start their own garden elsewhere. I see the effect of the community garden as a stone thrown into water – even a small stone causes countless ripples. Our community garden is not large, but its influence reaches quite far. We regularly organise open days and my favourite thing to hear a visitor say is: 'I could do that in my backyard too!'

EXAMPLES OF PLANTING

In order to make best use of the limited space, we plant our square beds very intensively, with two or three crops every season. This way, we are able to harvest something from the garden even in the middle of winter. It helps that the garden is in the middle of the city where winter temperatures are milder and that the surrounding buildings shelter it from strong winds. At the beginning of every season, we add a layer of our home-made compost or well-rotted manure to every bed and fresh woodchip to the paths. Over the years, I developed several plantings that can neatly follow each other up during the season. Apart from the plantings below, we also grow other vegetables in the half-sized narrow beds, such as carrots, beets, chard, spring onions and early potatoes. One of the beds is permanently devoted to a mix of perennial herbs.

Checkerboard lettuce bed

Bed 1

lettuce + kale

April: 16 lettuce plants

In April, we set the lettuce out 25cm (10in) apart. We usually grow romaine or loose-leaf lettuces and I like to plant them in a checkerboard pattern, alternating green and red plants. We harvest the lettuce 'leaf-by-leaf' which spreads the harvest over many weeks.

June: 9 kale plants

Because the kale is planted at a different spacing than lettuce, it can be planted before the lettuce has finished. When the lettuce starts bolting, we take the plants out and the kale gets ample space to bulk up. Around September/ October we start harvesting the kale, in the same way we picked the lettuce. It regrows slowly throughout the winter and then picks up again in early spring. When the plants start bolting we pick a final harvest of the flowers and then pull the plants out to make space for the next crop.

Bed 2

spinach + courgette + rocket and corn salad

March: 6 rows of spinach

The spinach is sown directly as soon as the soil warms up a bit. It can be harvested repeatedly as a cut-and-come-again crop, by cutting the leaves about 2.5cm (1in) above ground.

May: 1 courgette

Around mid-May we plant a courgette in the middle of the bed. That does not mean all the spinach has to come out: a little space in the middle is enough at the beginning. As the courgette grows, the spinach has to make more space until the courgette takes over the whole bed. We harvest the courgette fruits small to stimulate the plant to keep producing.

September: 10 rows of rocket and corn salad

When the courgette plant starts looking tired, we take it out and sow hardy salads. Both of these can be harvested repeatedly. Corn salad is hardy enough to withstand just about any Dutch winter weather; rocket will only survive in mild winters. In March/ April they start to bolt and it's time to remove them.

Bed 3
broad beans + leeks

March: 25 broad beans

Broad beans are fairly hardy which is why they can be sown early, sometimes already in February, 20cm (8in) apart in both directions. Because most varieties grow quite tall, they appreciate some kind of support. We put a bamboo cane in every corner of the bed and span twine between the canes, also diagonally across the bed. As members of the legume family, broad beans leave nitrogen in the soil which can benefit the following crop.

July: leeks

We sow leeks in March or April in one of our narrow little beds. In July, when the broad beans have finished, we transplant the leeks into the bed, 20cm apart. For planting, I use a dibber to make a 15-20cm (6-8in) deep hole in the ground, then drop the young leek plant into it and water thoroughly. Over time, the hole fills up with earth and the bottom part of the leek is blanched in the process. We harvest the leeks from fall onwards, alternating between plants in a row so that the distance between the remaining plants gradually increases and they can grow even bigger.

Bed 4
sugar snaps/snow peas + endive

March/April: sugar snap peas and/or snow peas

In March we erect a willow tipi or make a simpler (but also less pretty) one from bamboo canes. When the soil has warmed up, we sow the peas, about 5cm (2in) apart. The tipi serves as a support for the growing plants but sometimes they need to be tied to it with a string. When the pods appear, we pick them regularly to make sure the plants keep flowering and forming new pods.

August: 20 curled endive plants

Endive pre-sown in July is ready for transplanting about a month later, after the peas have finished. Just like broad beans, peas are capable of fixing nitrogen from the air and leave some behind in the soil. A leafy vegetable such as endive needs sufficient nitrogen to grow well and will therefore benefit from the nitrogen left behind.

Bed 5
radishes and leaf mustard + tomatoes + winter purslane

March: 10 rows of radishes and leaf mustard

These fast-growing spring vegetables give us an early harvest: radishes are harvested whole (the young leaves are tasty too and can be stir fried); the leaf mustard is harvested as a cut-and-come-again salad and will provide several cuttings.

May: 4 tomato plants

After mid-May, we plant four tomatoes, immediately adding a bamboo cane for support. We prefer indeterminate cultivars with some disease resistance, even though thanks to the community garden being quite isolated from other gardens, plants tend to remain relatively healthy. We remove side shoots regularly to keep the plants in check and harvest the fruits as they ripen. A few basil plants can be planted on the south side of the bed.

September: winter purslane

After the tomato plants are finished, or if they keep on fruiting into the fall, even before that, we sow winter purslane – either in rows or broadcasting seed all over the bed. As this is one of the hardiest salad plants, which regrows even in low light levels, we can usually keep harvesting it well into spring. Winter purslane too can be treated as a cut-and-come-again crop.

Risotto is one of those universal dishes in which you can use just about any vegetable. At the beginning of summer, I like to make it with a colourful mix of baby vegetables, the result of 'harvest-thinning'. The risotto in the photo was made with vegetables harvested from the community garden on a beautiful day in June.

There's a possible shortcut to this recipe: instead of pre-cooking each vegetable separately you can cook them directly in the risotto, adding them towards the end of the cooking time. But this only works if they're very fresh and tender and you're sure of your timing.

Baby vegetable risotto

Approx. 1.5 litres (6 cups) vegetable stock
1 tbsp olive oil
1 tbsp butter
1 medium onion, finely chopped
2 cloves of garlic, finely chopped
500g (2 cups) risotto rice
150ml (⅔ cup) red wine (but white wine is fine too, I just like the pinkish colour here)
About 400g (1lb) assorted baby vegetables (small carrots, small beets with their greens, snow peas or sugar snaps, tiny broad beans)
2 spring onions
1 tbsp finely chopped tarragon or parsley
1 tbsp butter
1 handful of grated Parmesan cheese, plus more to serve

Cut larger vegetables in bite-sized pieces, but leave tiny ones whole to show them off. Roughly chop the leaves of the beets and finely slice the spring onions.

In a medium pan, bring water to a boil, then add carrots. Cook until just tender, about five minutes. Remove and cook the rest of the vegetables separately until tender too. The beets might need a little longer, snow peas only about two minutes. Set the cooked vegetables apart.

Have your stock simmering on the stove.

Heat the butter and oil in a wide skillet. Add the onion and cook over medium heat until softened, about four minutes. Add the garlic and after another minute add the rice. Turn up the heat, stirring continuously until the rice begins to look translucent, about two minutes. Add the wine and stir until it's absorbed.

Turn the heat down a bit: it should be just high enough to maintain a lively bubble. Begin adding the stock, one ladle at a time, adding more after the stock has been absorbed and stirring continuously.

When the rice is almost done (after about 15 minutes), and you have about two ladles of stock left, add the lightly cooked vegetables, the chopped beet leaves and spring onions. Add the last stock and cook for three more minutes.

Turn off the heat, stir in the butter, tarragon (or parsley) and Parmesan and cover the pot. Let sit for a couple of minutes, then check the seasoning.

Serve with a little freshly grated Parmesan on top.

Potager

Permaculture gardening is often associated with irregularly shaped beds and seemingly chaotic planting but I think that it is perfectly possible to create a full-blown ornamental kitchen garden while still adhering to the trio of the most important principles: 1) no digging, 2) mulching and 3) diversity. The one huge advantage of an ornamental vegetable garden is that it will more likely earn a prime spot close to the house, be it in the front yard or adjacent to your terrace. A garden that is in full view from the house (and maybe also from the houses of your neighbours or passers-by) is much more likely to receive the attention needed to make it a success. As Robert Kourik puts it: 'Plant your vegetables no farther from the house than you can throw the kitchen sink.'

Several years ago I set out to create a small potager within our larger vegetable garden, mainly for fun but also to test some planting ideas. I also wanted to show that a vegetable garden can be productive and beautiful for most of the year as well as low maintenance and sustainable at the same time. It is true that an ornamental kitchen garden takes a little more thought and effort to create but in my experience, this will be repaid with increased productivity. The more beautiful a garden is, the more time you'll want to spend there and the better you will care for it. You'll likely water it properly, pull out any weeds as soon as they emerge and harvest every crop when it's at its best. For the two years we had it, our little potager was not only the most admired but also the best maintained and consequently the most productive part of our kitchen garden.

THE DESIGN

Though it is possible to create an irregularly shaped ornamental vegetable garden, most classic potagers rely on simple geometric patterns, their beauty arising from symmetry and repetition. My potager was 3m wide and 5m long (10 x 16.5ft) and I chose a simple design with two crossing paths and a diamond-shaped bed in the middle (this bed could also be round). It is important not to forget the practical side of things: all paths should be a minimum of 30cm (1ft) wide but I prefer mine a little wider. For a more permanent design and a more formal look, the beds could be edged with wood, tiles, bricks or roof tiles and the paths could be paved. Since our potager was a temporary experiment, I chose not to edge the beds and to cover the paths with woodchip.

In traditional potagers, the paths are often lined with a low clipped box hedge, which gives the garden a well-defined structure throughout the year, even when the beds are mostly empty. But especially in a small garden, a permanent hedging takes up too much precious space. The established perennial plants compete with annual vegetables for moisture and nutrients, and it is time-consuming to keep the hedge neatly trimmed. I prefer to line my paths with low-growing vegetables or herbs. In this design, I chose colourful lettuce varieties and nasturtiums for the summer months and leaf mustard, pansies and chicories for autumn and winter. A tipi covered in runner beans added height to the garden. A more sturdy support (such as a tipi made of willow branches) could also support small-fruited winter squash varieties, such as the cute 'Jack-be-Little', green striped 'Sweet Dumpling' or an acorn squash.

THE PLANTING

To fill the beds, I chose vegetables that are relatively easy to grow in our climate, have an ornamental value and are delicious when freshly picked such as lettuce, edible flowers and young beets. Only healthy plants look pretty, which is why I excluded tomatoes, for example, that are difficult to keep disease-free in our rainy climate. Instead, I planted chillies and aubergines that do not mind excessive moisture. It is important to choose varieties that are suitable to your climate though; aubergine 'Early Black Egg' is one of the earliest ripening varieties and will usually provide a decent harvest even in our short Dutch summers. These days, seed companies offer a plethora of colourful varieties of even the most common vegetables, which inspired me to play with colour in my design and plant the beds to the left with mostly red and purple vegetables and those to the right with orange and red.

In order to keep the garden constantly full, it is in most cases better to start with transplants instead of sowing crops directly. For a seamless transition between summer and autumn planting, chard and kale can be planted shortly after midsummer among the other plants. For the remaining crops you'll need to wait until there's more space available.

As I mentioned earlier, repetition is an important part of the design and that poses the biggest challenge of an ornamental planting: how to have your cake and eat it too? As soon as you harvest a head of lettuce, for example, a hole will emerge in the carefully designed planting. This is the reason why you'll often encounter potagers where nothing much is actually harvested for fear of spoiling the

picture. In my opinion though, ornamental or not, providing produce to eat remains the kitchen garden's raison d'être. If you cleverly employ some of the aforementioned harvesting techniques, you can prevent empty spots and make sure your garden remains pretty even though you're harvesting from it regularly. Lettuce, chard and kale can be picked leaf-by-leaf, instead of harvesting whole plants. Basil, as well as perilla, are best harvested by repeatedly cutting the tops and letting the plants branch out and grow further. Both the leaves and flowers of nasturtiums can be harvested as needed and picking the flowers regularly will keep the plants flowering longer. Beets can be planted (or sown) quite close together and repeatedly harvest-thinned. The last ones will be picked early September, just in time for sowing a few rows of hardy mustard leaves. The mustard can either be picked leaf-by-leaf or as a 'cut-and-come-again'.

How beautiful and bountiful the potager will be in winter depends largely on the weather. Kale, leeks and winter purslane are hardy enough to withstand our typical winters. Chicory and chard will not survive long periods of severe frost in combination with lots of moisture, but if the winter is mild and dry, they'll keep going.

Both lettuce and edible flowers can be repeatedly harvested without destroying the design

Potager planting for summer

Yellow-orange borders

Lettuce 'Crisp mint' and 'Australian Yellow'
Beet 'Burpee's Golden'
Pepper 'Bulgarian Carrot'
Basil 'Genovese'
Nasturtium 'Salmon Baby'
Chard 'Golden'
Kale 'Dwarf Green Curled'

Red-purple borders

Lettuce 'Pablo Picasso' and red oakleaf
Beet 'Sanguina'
Aubergine 'Early Black Egg'
Red perilla (or purple basil)
Nasturtium 'Empress of India'
Chard 'Ruby Red'
Kale 'Red Ursa'

Diamond-shaped bed

Tipi with runner beans 'Sunrise' surrounded by lettuce 'Red Velvet' (can be interplanted with nasturtiums)

Potager planting for autumn/winter

Yellow-orange borders

Rows of mustard 'Yellow frills' and 'Pizzo' (as cut-and-come-again)
Leek 'Hannibal'
Kale 'Dwarf Green Curled'
Chard 'Golden'
Orange winter pansies
Kohlrabi 'White Delicacy'
Chicory 'Grumolo Verde'

Red-purple borders

Rows of mustard 'Red Frills' and 'Red Giant'
Leek 'St. Victor'
Kale 'Red Ursa'
Chard 'Ruby Red'
Purple pansies
Kohlrabi 'Blue Delicatesse'
Chicory 'Di Verona'

Diamond-shaped bed

Early sprouting broccoli surrounded by winter purslane or corn salad or alternating red and green chicories

MIXING IT UP

In the previous three examples, the plantings got progressively more complex with a higher degree of diversity. The beginner's garden had just a handful of crops; in the community garden different crops followed each other within a season and in the potager many were combined within fairly orderly beds. But several years ago, inspired by the polycultures described by Toby Hemenway in his book *Gaia's Garden*, I started to experiment with a more radical way of mixing crops together.

Small-scale polyculture

My goal in developing the following polyculture was to maximise the yield from a very limited space while being able to enjoy a variety of crops. Vegetables such as courgette or cabbages were discounted on account of the amount of space they take up. I chose crops that could be sown all at the same time but harvested over a long period of time, from the first mustard green seedlings which I pick just three and a half weeks after sowing, to parsnips that we enjoy until the following spring. Because there is also a difference in how fast different varieties within each group grow, the harvest is spread evenly over many months. This is why, for example, I sow several different varieties of lettuce and include both early and late varieties of carrots. The huge diversity of the planting is firstly possible

The polyculture in July: harvesting carrots, beets and chard

thanks to succession: leaf mustard is the first to germinate and the first to be harvested, making room for the other crops. Secondly, the vegetables can also grow very close together because they have different root systems and need different nutrients from the soil. The diversity in growth habit helps too: the slender upright leaves of spring onions and feathery leaves of carrots fit easily among crops that have a more ground-hugging growth habit such as lettuce and chicory.

Starting in spring, the ground is continually covered with plants. Within a few weeks, the fast-growing mustards form a living mulch and keep the soil moist so that the slow-germinating crops such as carrots and parsnips can germinate well too. Because the bed is never bare, the soil does not dry out as quickly and watering does not need to be as frequent. Besides, this living mulch discourages weeds and very little weeding is needed throughout the season.

In the first year I grew this polyculture I sowed it on just about two square metres. Even in this limited space, the harvest was huge: between 9th May and 10th July (when we left for our holiday), we harvested 6.7kg (14lb 12oz) of mixed salads. Considering the average supermarket bag of mixed leaves is around 100g (3.5oz), this would be the equivalent of 67 bags of mixed salads, enough to provide a daily serving of salad for our family. But unlike the supermarket salads which offer pretty much the same boring mix all year round, the composition of our salads changed from week to week: from mustard greens to lettuce to chicories with some edible flowers and herbs thrown in. Because we were growing more salads elsewhere in the garden, it actually got to a point where I was giving bags of mixed leaves to other mums when picking up our kids from school.

The polyculture less than five weeks after sowing: harvesting mustard greens and lettuce at seedling stage

THE CROPS IN MY POLYCULTURE

Below I list the varieties I have grown in my polycultures over the years, but there are of course many others you could include, depending on your personal preference and availability of seed. Either way, it is a good idea to sow a few different varieties from every group. To reduce cost, you can also buy seed mixes – mustards, lettuce, carrots and even chicories are often available as a mix of varieties. The polyculture can also be an opportunity to use old leftover seeds with uncertain germination rates. For carrots, parsnips and parsley though, because the seeds lose viability fast, it is probably a good idea to use some fresh seed as well. The groups are listed in the order in which I like to sow them. The first group (mustard greens) is the one I sow at the highest density, because it can be harvested early and we eat a relatively large amount of it. The following groups are sown at progressively lower density because the crops will usually need more space to reach a harvestable stage. It is difficult to be exact when broadcasting seed, but try to aim for approximately one seed per very 2.5 x 2.5cm ($1in^2$). But do not get too anxious about it – if you sow too densely, you can later correct that by harvesting more aggressively.

Since you need to be able to recognise the different crops at seedling stage, this polyculture might not be suited for a beginning gardener. However, if you are just starting and do want to try it, I would suggest you opt for strikingly coloured varieties. Within most of the groups listed below you can find varieties with either red, purple or yellow-coloured leaves which will make distinguishing between your seedlings and weeds much easier.

Mustard greens (*Brassicaceae*)

Mustard greens can usually be harvested for the first time within four weeks after sowing. There are many varieties available with different shapes of leaves and in different colours, some tasting quite hot and some milder. To save money and make things simpler, you can also buy a mixed seed packet.

I like to sow any of the following: Rocket, Bekana, Mizuna, Purple mizuna, Golden Streaks, Ruby Streaks, Golden Frills, Scarlet Frills, Osaka Purple, Pink Lettucy, Pizzo.

Lettuce (*Compositae*)

Don't just sow the classic butterhead, but include other types of lettuce too, such as iceberg and cos that take longer to mature, to prolong the harvest. Most lettuce plants will be harvested before they are fully grown, but you can let a few get bigger and form hearts. The miniature lettuces such as 'Little Gem' or 'Tom Thumb' are best suited for that. The varieties below are just a few I like to grow but feel free to vary the mix or buy a readymade one.

Buttercrunch, Mottistone, Pablo Picasso, Claremont, Pinokkio, Catalogna Cerbiatta, Flashy Butter Oak, Little Gem.

Endive and Chicory (*Compositae*)

There are both leaf varieties and hearting varieties and it is a good idea to sow both. The leaf varieties (such as 'Zuccherina di Triestre') are faster growing and can be picked early in the season, while the hearting varieties grow slowly and can often be harvested well into winter (depending on the weather). Among the hearting cultivars are the many beautiful varieties of radicchio with deep purple or streaked leaves. I often opt for a readymade mix in this case, but below are a few suggestions.

Zuccherina di Triestre (leaf chicory), Grumolo Verde (green rosette of leaves), Palla Rossa (hearting red), Castefranco (variegated hearting), Di Treviso (tall red hearting), Catalogna Frastagliata (resembles dandelion and can be cut several times).

Onions (*Alliaceae*)

The slender spring onions are well suited to be grown among other plants and are reasonably fast growing. Alliums are also beneficial for the overall health of the polyculture, since they have antibacterial and antifungal properties. I like to grow one white and one red/purple variety, but otherwise it is not necessary to sow many different ones in this case.

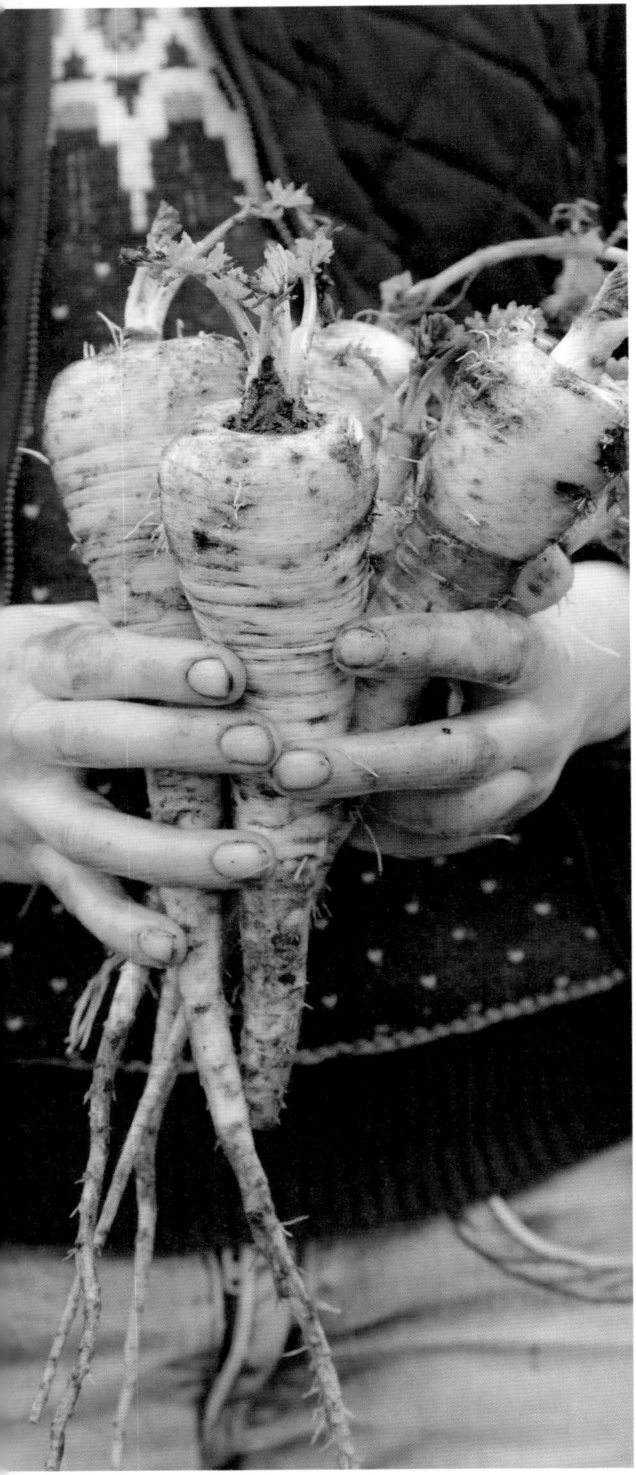

Parsnips harvested in March the next year

I have grown many: White: White Lisabon (quick growing and also quite hardy), Ishikura (slender and fast growing), Shimonita Negi (thick stems and sweet taste).

Purple: Apache (deep purple-red and mild flavoured), Red Beard (pretty pink).

Roots (Umbelliferae)

I like to include both an early and a late carrot variety to prolong the harvest and I also like to throw in a purple coloured one with a high antioxidant content. The slowly maturing but very hardy parsnips can be harvested throughout the winter, as long as the soil is not frozen.

Some varieties I've grown in my polycultures: Bambino (fast maturing baby carrot variety), Nantes 2 (early blunt-ended variety with some carrot fly resistance), Cosmic Purple (sweet purple maincrop carrot), Autumn King (high-yielding maincrop variety), parsnip Tender and True or Guernsey Half Long.

Beets and chard (Chenopodiaceae)

Beets and chard belong to the same plant family, but are grown for different parts of the plant (even though the beet leaves are nice to eat too). Again, you can sow both early and late varieties of beets. As far as chard is concerned, it's better not to harvest the whole plant at once, but to keep picking the outer leaves as they keep regrowing. That way you keep the plant from becoming too large for the polyculture and prolong the harvest period.

I have grown: Beets: Boltardy (bolt-resistant), Flat of Egypt (very flavoursome), Di Chioggia (prettily striped), McGregor's Favourite (dual purpose beet grown both for its roots and the shiny ruby-red leaves), chard: Perpetual Spinach (hardier than the colourful varieties).

Herbs and edible flowers

Plants from this varied group attract beneficial insects and help to keep the polyculture healthy. Most of them self-sow in our garden.

Dill, parsley, heartsease, calendula, perilla.

POLYCULTURE IN NINE STEPS

1. Choose a site that is free of perennial weeds – preferably a site that has been cultivated for some time and well cared for during the previous season. This is really important because the seeds will be broadcasted instead of sown in rows, so weeding is not as easy.
2. Start sowing when the soil has warmed up in spring (in our climate that usually means somewhere in the first half of April). It is possible to start sowing a little earlier (towards the end of March) provided you protect the bed with a row cover.
3. Sow the seeds per group, e.g. mix the seeds of all lettuce varieties in a small bowl and sow them together. If you were to mix all the seeds and sow everything at once, it would be very difficult to get an even distribution. The larger, heavy seeds would fall close by and the smaller, lighter seeds would land further away. Try to sow as evenly as possible and not too densely.
4. After sowing, cover the seedbed with a thin layer of weed-free compost. Most homemade compost contains weed seeds because it does not reach the temperature required to kill them. I usually use compost from our wormery, which is not only free of weed seeds but also very nutritious. If you do not have any reliable compost available, you can cover the bed with cocopeat for example.
5. Start harvesting as soon as the seedlings start getting crowded; do not wait till they are full grown. Harvest whole plants by cutting them just above soil level. Harvesting is also a way to correct an uneven distribution of plants: if there is a spot with a high density of seedlings, you need to harvest/thin more aggressively.
6. You can let several lettuce plants form hearts by giving them more room, i.e. harvesting the plants around them.
7. You can also leave a few plants of chard to grow longer and harvest them leaf-by-leaf. This way you will prolong the harvest and keep the size of the plants in check, so that they do not crowd out other crops.
8. Remove weeds as they appear and water the bed as necessary. However, because the soil is constantly covered by plants, neither should be necessary often.
9. Keep harvesting! Even if at some point the harvest is more than you can eat, keep removing plants so that the slower growing crops get enough room to develop further. Baby beets and carrots are a delicious treat, so harvest some when they are tiny and allow some to grow bigger.

Radicchio harvested in November

Large-scale polyculture

After the old conifer hedge next to the parking lot of our community centre was removed, there was an awkward strip of poor acidic soil left. To top things off, it was also riddled with horsetail, a very persistent perennial weed. The board of the community centre asked our community garden work group whether we would be interested in taking it on, since we'd already proven our capabilities on the little plot behind the football cage. At that point, the spot was far from ideal for growing vegetables, so we decided to use clearance mulch for the first season (2013) and grow in straw bales. After covering the soil with large pieces of cardboard, we put a row of straw bales down the middle and mulched around them with woodchip to cover the unsightly cardboard. The bales were conditioned to start the composting process and later planted with different vegetables, herbs and strawberries. Needless to say, our straw bale garden attracted a lot of attention and I even heard of a few people attempting the technique in their own garden. At the beginning of 2014 we had a mostly weed-free plot measuring roughly 2 x 13m (6ft6in x 42ft) and several partially composted straw bales. The time was ripe for a new experiment.

After the success of my small-scale polyculture, I was eager to try one that could include larger vegetables such as squash, cabbages and corn as well. Because this garden would be the first thing the visitors to the community centre would see, it was important for it to also look attractive. Luckily, a diverse polyculture is always more interesting to look at than rows of just one vegetable.

Once again, I used the well-known 'three sisters' polyculture, a combination of corn, beans and squash grown by Native Americans, as my inspiration. But since I wanted more variety in my planting, I also added cabbages, courgette, tomatoes, onions, chard, herbs and edible flowers. The variety in planting meant a varied harvest that provided an overall bigger yield than if only one crop was grown. The harvest was also conveniently spread out over the course of many months – from the first courgettes in June to the kale and cabbages that could be picked in winter, winter squash that could be stored for many months and beans that could be dried for later.

Since the soil was poor and many of the vegetables we were planning to grow were heavy feeders, we used another local resource to improve the soil: manure from the neighbour's pony and goats that he was only too glad to get rid of. In addition to the compost we make in our community garden it supplied the much needed organic matter as well as nutrients. On top of the manure, we spread the half-composted straw, which would reduce evaporation and prevent weed growth, and the garden was ready for planting.

I started most of the crops (with the exception of onions and beans) at home on the windowsill, so that they would be ready for planting out around mid-May, after our average last frost date. Some of the vegetables are hardy (cabbages, chard and onions) and could be planted out earlier, but I prefer the convenience of planting everything at once. In the beginning, the vegetables seemed quite far apart, but they soon filled the available space. The resulting garden was colourful and abundant and became a real eye-catcher and an advertisement for 'grow-your-own'.

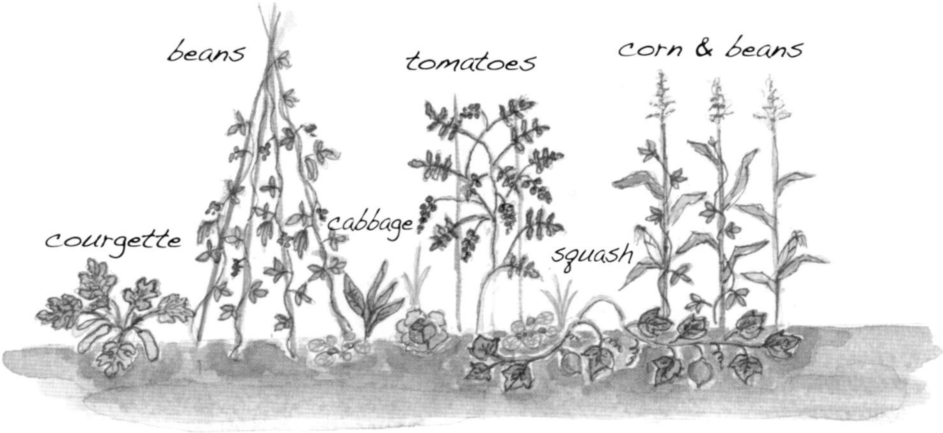

THE DESIGN

In order to make the best use of the available space, tall crops (tomatoes, corn and climbing beans) are alternated with low-growing, ground-covering crops. My design is meant for a 1 x 5m (3 x 16ft) bed but can easily be adjusted for a smaller or a bigger plot. Because the strip we had available was longer (about 13m total), we just repeated the planting in the same order and ended up with three bean tipis, two tomato plants and two groups of corn. If you have less than 5m available, for example just 3m, you can simplify the design and grow beans on one end of the bed, a group of corn on the other, with a courgette, a winter squash or cabbages and chard in between.

To prevent the tall crops from casting too much shade over the low crops, the bed should be oriented in the north-south direction. For easy maintenance and harvesting, it is also important that it can be accessed from both sides. If you want to grow the same polyculture on the same plot in subsequent years (as we have been doing for several years now), it is wise to move the design a bit to prevent the same crops (especially tomatoes and cabbages) from growing in exactly the same spot year after year. Moving it also means a different vegetable can profit from the nitrogen left behind in the soil by the beans.

THE CROPS

Unlike in the previous polyculture, most of the crops in this one will not be harvested as a whole plant. An exception to this is the cabbages but even these can be left to regrow. The rest are mostly fruit vegetables that can be picked over a long period of time – this way the garden will keep looking nice and full for most of the season.

Most of these vegetables can be bought as plants, so even if it's May and you have not sown a thing, you could still buy transplants and get this garden going. The advantage of starting plants from seed yourself is that you can choose from many more varieties.

The tall plants

Climbing beans

Beans are the only crop in the polyculture that we sow directly. Contrary to other seeds, the large bean seeds can be successfully sown in the straw mulch. But to get a bit of a head start, beans too can be started indoors and planted out after mid-May, together with the rest.

In the polyculture, beans appear twice: grown up a tipi and also together with the corn. In the first case, we use either bamboo canes or willow for support, in the second the beans wind themselves around the corn stalks. We grow a different variety of climbing bean per tipi, but if you only have one tipi, you could also sow different varieties around it. We always grow at least one variety of runner bean (*Phaseolus coccineus*) because it can be harvested at many different stages. First we enjoy some of the flowers in salads, then we pick some green pods whole before the seeds start swelling and lastly we harvest the seeds, either to eat fresh or to let them dry for the winter. Other varieties we've enjoyed growing (and eating) are borlotti beans 'Lingua di Fuoco' or interesting heirlooms such as 'Cave Pole' bean.

Tomatoes

In our wet climate, tomatoes are not easy to grow outside. I have tried many supposedly blight-resistant varieties over the years and in my experience, it is those that are the closest to the wild species that are least prone to disease. For this polyculture, I like to grow 'Orange Currant' and 'Matt's Wild Cherry'. Their fruits are on the small side (especially in the case of the 'Orange Currant') but they are both very productive varieties.

The plants are unruly and do not take well to being pruned to a single stem, so we put a couple of canes around them with a string tied all around to support the plants. A cage made out of garden mesh would be a good alternative. Even in very wet summers, the plants usually remain healthy and continue to produce fruits till October.

Corn

Because corn is pollinated by wind, it should never be planted in a single row. In the polyculture we plant a group of nine plants in a grid, with 45cm between the plants in both directions. When the plants are about

20cm tall, we sow two beans next to each corn plant. We usually grow sweet corn since that is everybody's favourite and such a treat when eaten absolutely fresh. Among the heirlooms, 'Golden Bantam' is delicious and fairly easy to grow in our climate. The bicoloured 'Double Standard' with white and yellow kernels has also done well. But sometimes we also grow double sweet or super sweet varieties such as 'Early Xtra Sweet' and 'Conqueror', which keep their sweet taste much longer. Something to bear in mind: pollination by corn that is grown as fodder for livestock or for flour can result in loss of sweetness in sweet corn varieties. Likewise, super sweet corn will be negatively affected if it is pollinated by other varieties. To prevent this, you can try to stagger the flowering times by sowing some varieties later.

American Spider Flower

According to some sources, Native Americans added the closely related *Cleome serrulata* (bee-spider flower) to their polyculture as a fourth 'sister' to attract pollinators. In our polyculture, we grow *Cleome hassleriana* that fulfils the same function but also makes a beautiful, long-lasting cut flower. It is available in white, pink and purple, but personally I enjoy the purple variety 'Violet Queen' the most.

The low plants

Cabbages

Any cabbages can be used and we usually put in a mix of Chinese, Savoy and red cabbages plus some kale to guarantee a varied harvest over a long period of time. The strong scent of the neighbouring tomato helps to confuse the many pests cabbages tend to attract. Kale can be harvested leaf-by-leaf and the other cabbages can be left to grow small secondary heads after the initial harvest.

Courgette

There are many varieties of courgette: dark green, pale green, yellow, striped, round... One variety that has done particularly well in our polyculture was 'Cavili', a hybrid that can set fruit even without pollination which means it produces lots of fruits even in relatively cool summers. The downside is that you cannot save your own seed. I am willing to compromise since during the wet and cold summer of 2014 it produced at least twice as many fruits as other courgette varieties, starting in June and carrying on until November. If you'd rather have an open-pollinated variety, 'Black Beauty' is reliable and delicious.

Winter squash

The vines of trailing winter squash weave themselves among the other plants, covering the soil and only needing to be moved gently if they grow out of the bed. For suggestions for varieties see Chapter 4 but one that we often plant here is the orange 'Uchiki Kuri'. One year we also planted the mini-pumpkin 'Gold Speck' and let it climb up the barbed wire at the back.

Chard

The leaves of this versatile plant can be used as spinach but unlike spinach, chard does not bolt as soon as the weather warms up and so it can be harvested much longer. We usually grow the green variety with narrow stems, also known as 'perpetual spinach', but any of the colourful varieties such as 'Ruby Red' or 'Golden Sunrise' would be equally good here and would provide a splash of colour as well.

Basil

Among the cabbages and around the tomatoes there are two varieties of basil: the classic Genovese and 'Dark Opal', a pretty purple variety. The strong scent protects other vegetables from pests and the small flowers attract bees.

Nasturtium

The peppery taste of the flowers makes nasturtiums deservedly one of the most popular edible flowers and it is also a good companion plant. Because in this case, nasturtiums are meant for the understory of the polyculture, I choose the compact dwarf varieties instead of some of the more rampant ones. Any variety will do but one of my favourites 'Princess of India', with its deep red flowers and dark leaves, contrasts beautifully with other crops.

Onion

Dotted throughout the bed we plant a few onions – their antifungal properties make them a useful member of any polyculture. If planted too late, onions will not form substantial bulbs, but you can harvest the green parts repeatedly – often they will even re-sprout in spring.

Irma, one of the volunteers, harvesting from the polyculture

VARIATION IN THE PLANTING

Instead of (or in addition to) the above-mentioned crops, you can plant other ones as well. If you enjoy experimenting with lesser-known edibles, then you could for example grow a group of quinoa (*Chenopodium quinoa*) plants as one of the tall crops. You can sow in rows about 25cm (10in) apart and thin to a group of 12-16 plants. Quinoa is very productive, highly nutritious and much easier to grow and process than more traditional grains (botanically speaking it is not really a grain but related to spinach and beetroot). Another option is yacon (*Smallanthus sonchifolius*), a plant from the Andes, producing sizable juicy and crunchy tubers that we mostly enjoy raw. Sunflowers, which produce edible seeds or can be picked as cut flowers, are a pretty addition and can also serve as a support for climbing beans. For the low crops, consider another South-American tuber, oca (*Oxalis tuberosa*). The yield in our climate is much smaller than in the case of yacon, but the plants are pretty and the leaves are edible too. Both yacon and oca are best started in pots inside before planting them out together with the other plants.

This lovely summer dish is made almost exclusively with produce from the polyculture (even more so if you also grow quinoa in it!).

Stuffed courgettes

2 medium sized courgettes
100g (⅔ cup) quinoa
1 tbsp olive oil
1 small onion, minced
1 clove of garlic, minced
Kernels from 1 ear of sweet corn
350g (12oz) cherry tomatoes, halved
Handful of basil, leaves roughly chopped
50g (2oz) Parmesan cheese, finely grated

First, prepare the courgettes: cut them in half horizontally, then scoop out the flesh using a small knife and a spoon, leaving an edge of about 8mm (⅓in). Reserve the flesh. Sprinkle the inside with salt and let the halves drain (upside down) on a clean tea towel to get rid of as much moisture as possible.

Meanwhile, preheat the oven to 180°C (360°F) and prepare the filling. Boil the quinoa according to package instructions. Heat the olive oil in a large skillet, add the onion and sauté until translucent. Add the garlic, sweet corn and roughly chopped courgette flesh. Sauté for about five minutes, then add the quinoa and tomatoes and sauté for a couple more minutes. Take the pan from the heat and stir in the basil and Parmesan. Rub the insides of the courgettes with a little olive oil and fill to capacity with the quinoa mix. Bake in the preheated oven until the courgette is done (check by piercing the flesh with the point of a knife) and the filling starts to brown lightly on top, about 30 minutes.

THEMED POLYCULTURES

Apart from all the other benefits of polycultures, I believe they are also an opportunity to get creative and be playful which is why I sometimes create small, one-bed polycultures organised around a certain theme. Last year I created two such beds: a Mexican polyculture and one planted with Oriental vegetables. I hope these two examples will encourage you to try your hand at designing your own!

Mexican polyculture

Sometimes, especially on one of the many dreary days in our seemingly endless winters, I wonder what it would be like to live in a different climate. For example in Mexico, where it's always warm, the sun shines far more regularly and gardens can be abundant and colourful all year round. My family also very much enjoys the lively tastes of Mexican cuisine and dishes like tacos and vegetarian chilli often appear on the menu. Last year I decided to bring a little Mexico into my garden and planted one of my raised beds with a colourful mix of vegetables, herbs and flowers that hail from the Americas.

Obviously our climate poses some limitations and those determined the crops and varieties I could grow and the way I grew them. Our summers are relatively short which means it is necessary to start tender crops inside, in our case on a sunny windowsill. The first crop to be sown was the chilli peppers, which I started at the end of February. In the second half of March I sowed the tomatillos and in April the rest of the plants. After mid-May, when the soil was warm and frost no longer threatened, I planted everything out. In order to prevent the tall crops (corn and sunflowers) from shading the rest of the plants, I planted those at the north side of the bed. In front of them I planted the tomatillos and at the front of the bed the chillies and herbs with a few zinnias tucked in. In total, there were eight different crops in my one bed, spanning five plant families – an excellent way to prevent disease and pest problems!

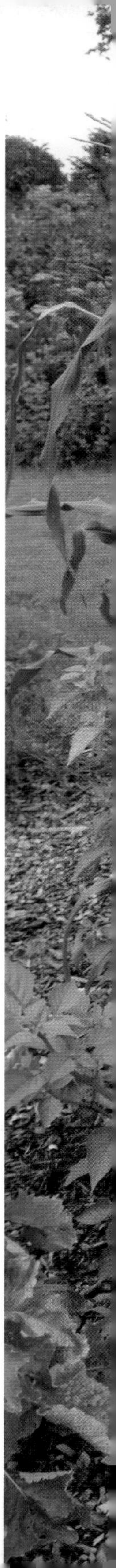

Corn (*Zea mays*)

What wheat is to us, corn is to Mexicans. For centuries, it has been a staple of their diet and the indigenous inhabitants still sometimes refer to themselves as 'corn people'. However, it is not ordinary sweet corn they allude to – most of the corn grown in Mexico is ground to flour and used for making traditional dishes such as tortillas and tamales. To honour this, I chose a variety called 'Painted Mountain' which can be eaten fresh when very young but is best dried and ground into flour. It also happens to be very beautiful and if you do not eat all of it, you can use the ears as fall décor. Since it is a variety bred in Montana, it is better suited to our climate than truly Mexican varieties would be. To dry the corn, I hang the ears in a warm and dry place. When the kernels are completely dry, they can easily be rubbed off and stored in a glass jar. If you have a real grain mill, it will work great, but grinding small quantities in a handheld coffee grinder has worked well for me too. Nine or 16 plants can be planted on a grid, the wider spacing preferable if you also want a decent harvest of beans from plants that will climb up the stalks.

Runner bean (*Phaseolus coccineus*)

To stay with the theme, I chose runner beans with red flowers and multi-coloured seeds to grow next to my corn. Beans were the only crop that was direct-sown and I sowed them in the same way as in the previous polyculture: two beans next to each corn plant when the plants were about 20cm (8in) tall. The bean plants will not give you a huge harvest (especially if you choose the closer spacing for the corn) but since they do not really take up any extra space, why not add them?

Tomatillo (*Physalis ixocarpa*)

Tomatillo belongs to the same botanical family as tomato (the nightshades) and I grow them in the same way: pre-sowing inside in March and planting out in May. But since tomatillo is much less prone to fungal disease, it is a lot easier to grow outside in our rainy climate. The plants are sprawling and extremely productive – two or three are usually enough for our family. The fruits can be green or purple and are covered in a paper-like husk that opens when the fruits are ripe. We use them to make an authentic 'salsa verde' and at the end of the season I preserve the last fruits in a tomatillo chutney.

Chilli pepper (*Capsicum annuum*)

Mexican cuisine is unimaginable without the heat of chillies and the Mexicans are true connoisseurs who appreciate the distinctive

flavours and varying degrees of hotness in different varieties. Unfortunately, many of the types of chillies popular in Mexico (such as habanero, serrano or poblano) need more heat to ripen than our climate will provide and could only be successfully grown in a greenhouse. For growing outside, I like the reliable 'Westland Long Red' which gives us a decent harvest even during mediocre summers. Admittedly not authentic but still a good condiment for many dishes. Before the first frost, I gather all the remaining fruits, thread them on a string and hang them in our living room to dry. During the winter, whenever I need a chilli for a dish, I just snip one off.

Mexican marigold (*Tagetes lucida*)

In its warm country of origin, Mexican marigold is a perennial plant, but because it is not hardy, we grow it as an annual. Unlike in the ornamental marigolds often used as bedding, the flowers of Mexican marigold are quite small and subtle and only appear towards the end of the season. It is not for the flowers we grow it though but for the aromatic leaves. The taste is reminiscent of tarragon with distinct notes of aniseed. In Mexican cuisine it is paired with corn, squash or poultry, but our favourite way to enjoy it is as a tisane. The leaves can be dried for use in winter.

Mexican giant hyssop and Anise hyssop (*Agastache mexicana* and *A. foeniculum*)

Anise hyssop belongs to the mint family and has a pleasant aniseed flavour. Both the leaves and the flowers can be used for a refreshing herbal tea or in fruit salads. The plant has medicinal properties too – it can be used to fight fever and cough. But there is one more reason why I added it to my polyculture: it is an excellent pollinator attractant. This plant is actually a perennial, so at the end of the season I replanted it in a sunny spot in the herb layer of my forest garden.

Sunflower (*Helianthus annuus*)

For the Aztecs, these happy flowers represented their sun god Huitzilopochtli and we too associate them with the sun. Apart from being a great cut flower, sunflowers are also edible: the seeds, the petals and the young leaves. You can also harvest the buds before they open (they resemble artichokes that belong to the same botanical family) and eat them lightly boiled with a bit of melted butter. Any flowers you do not pick, you can leave to develop seeds for birds that will be grateful for the nutritious snack. It is usually a good idea to give sunflowers some kind of support such as a bamboo cane. If you do not do that, they tend to become top-heavy and fall over.

Zinnias (*Zinnia*)

These beloved cut flowers too originated from Central America. The petals are edible but not terribly tasty and my main reason for adding them to my polyculture was to brighten up the bed and add some zest. Because I like to pick zinnias for the vase, I prefer the taller cultivars with sturdy stems, such as the Benary's Giant series. Regular picking ensures that the plants will keep flowering.

Oriental polyculture

Compared to the cuisine of Mexico, the cuisine of the countries of the Far East is rather understated and frugal – any edible part of a plant will be used. Many Oriental vegetables can, or often even prefer to, be sown later in the season (after midsummer) which means this polyculture can follow an early crop such as lettuce, broad beans or even early potatoes (if you start your plants in pots). Pretty much all of these plants fall into the 'unbuyable' category for me.

Celtuce (*Lactuca sativa* var. *asparagine*)

As soon as it gets really warm in summer, most lettuce will bolt. The leaves of most varieties will quickly get too bitter, but I usually salvage the crunchy stem, peeling it and snacking on it raw. But there is also a variety of lettuce that was bred especially to be used this way: celtuce. This lettuce never forms a head, but shoots up right away. The stem is also a lot thicker than that of regular bolted lettuce. Celtuce can withstand both colder and warmer temperatures than lettuce and can be started in March inside or sown outside from April till July. For my polyculture I sowed the variety 'Spring Tower' and I set the plants about 30cm (1ft) apart.

The best moment to harvest is just before the plants start running to flower, which is usually about three months after sowing, or when the lettuce is about 30-40cm tall (1ft-1ft4in). If you wait too long, the stem of the lettuce will become hollow. After harvesting, remove all leaves apart from the little rosette on top which helps to keep it fresh for longer. The leaves are of course edible too, but they are quite coarse compared to lettuce grown specifically for its leaves. If you're very frugally minded, you can prepare them like spinach, but I usually just throw them on the compost heap, since at that moment there are much more palatable leaves to be found in the garden. After peeling the outer layer, you can use the stem in different ways. My family prefers to eat the crunchy stem raw, so I either slice it thinly and add it to salads, or cut it in batons and serve those with a dip, in lieu of celery. I have also tried adding it to stir fries.

Edamame soya (*Glycine max*)

Most people are familiar with soya beans as a high-protein alternative to meat, but what they often don't realise is that they could actually be growing them in their garden, even if that garden is in a cool climate. However, soya beans are sensitive both to temperature and day length, so in order to be successful, we need to choose varieties that can handle our shorter season and will flower even in lower temperatures and during shorter days. In general, soya beans need more warmth

than regular bush beans, so if you want to sow directly, you'd better wait till the soil has really warmed up; in our climate that means sowing somewhere between the end of May and beginning of July. If starting the plants inside, you can push the date back by about a month. We grow the beans to eat fresh, not to dry, and for this they need to be picked after the pods have plumped up, but are still green. To shell the beans, you need to boil them in lightly salted water for about seven minutes – this makes the pods easier to open. The beans can then be used as a protein-rich addition to salads, stir fries or even puréed and seasoned to make a brightly green nutritious spread to use on bread.

Mizuna and mibuna (*Brassica rapa* var. *japonica*)

Two Oriental brassicas with a pleasant taste, milder than most mustard greens. The leaves of mibuna are long, narrow and dark green, while the leaves of mizuna are serrated and can be green or purple. Both can be grown at different spacing and harvested at different stages. In early spring, I often sow them close together for harvesting as cut-and-come-again seedlings, but for this polyculture I wanted full-grown plants, so I planted them further apart: 30cm (1ft). Mibuna and mizuna are in my experience more bolt-resistant than most of the other Oriental brassicas, but if they do bolt, we just eat the flowering shoots. In our household these two greens are mostly consumed raw, but in Japan they are often pickled. Both plants are also fairly hardy and I have grown them for winter cropping both in the greenhouse and under the protection of a cold frame.

Perilla or shiso (*Perilla frutescens*)

Sometimes nicknamed 'Oriental basil' this aromatic herb does not in fact resemble basil in taste, but it matches it in intensity and occupies a similarly central place in Japanese cuisine as basil does in the cuisine of Italy. The taste of perilla is not easy to describe, containing notes of cinnamon, cumin, citrus and coriander. In my experience, once you get perilla to germinate (which can be aided by putting the seed in the fridge for a week before sowing), the plants are very easy to grow, requiring less heat than basil and no special care. They are also quite ornamental, especially the red variety, and are therefore sometimes planted in flower borders. In Japan, shiso is used in countless different ways, among others in sushi, or to flavour both pickled ginger and umeboshi, the sour plum pickle. The flowering shoots or large leaves can be dipped in batter and fried as tempura. I often just simply add them whole to summer salads, like I do with mammoth basil.

Left: Celtuce

Edamame

Perilla

Miniature cut flower garden

Since I live in the Netherlands, the largest producer of cut flowers worldwide, growing my own flowers for cutting might seem like bringing coal to Newcastle. But because I do not like the way most of the flowers for the market are produced (forced in large-scale greenhouses and often sprayed liberally), I still prefer to grow flowers myself – organically. Besides, store-bought cut flowers can hardly compete with the easy charm and variety of flowers you can grow in your garden. Growing flowers will not only allow you to fill your vases and make your plot prettier, but many of them are also a great source of nectar for pollinators and attract beneficial insects into your garden. Even though growing food takes precedence over flowers for me, I have grown some flowers in every garden I've ever had. Depending on the overall size of my gardens in the past, I have devoted up to 100m² (1000ft²) to flowers – growing a huge variety of both annual and perennial ones. But in 2013, when we had to move from a 400m² (4300ft²) plot to one about three times smaller, I shrank my cut flower patch too, to just one bed. Like most of my other raised beds, this one was 1.2 x 3m (4 x 10ft), edged with wood and filled initially with homemade compost. Annual cut flowers are not heavy feeders and adding too much nitrogen, especially, would result in lush leaves at the expense of flowers. I tend to treat my flowers the same way I treat my vegetables: concentrating on improving the soil instead of feeding the plants and mulching to reduce evaporation and weed growth.

Because this bed (unlike most of my other beds) was oriented in a west-east direction, I could put a bamboo tipi in the middle of the bed without it shading the other plants too much. If I were planting in a north-south oriented bed, I would put the tipi on the north side of it. On both sides of the tipi, I planted the other tall plants: cosmos and American spider flower. The rest of the flowers were planted in groups to the left and to the right of those, with an average spacing of 25-30cm (10-12in). To obtain straight stems good for cutting and to stop the plants from falling over, I put in several short bamboo canes and spanned twine crisscross over the bed.

MY FAVOURITE ANNUAL CUT FLOWERS

Compared to perennials, annual cut flowers will (as long as you keep picking) usually flower over a much longer period of time. For the price of one or two store-bought bouquets, you can buy enough seeds to be able to grow and pick varied bouquets from your garden for at least four months of the year. Besides, you can tailor the bouquets to your preferences; some of my very favourite cut flowers such as the deliciously scented sweet pea 'Matucana' or tricoloured annual lupin 'Sunrise' can't be found in a flower shop. They might not be sturdy enough, not have the required stem length or have too short a vase life to be interesting for commercial cultivation. But if you can pick a fresh bouquet as often as you want and like tiny posies as well as large arrangements, none of this matters.

For my miniature cut flower garden, I wanted a big variety in a limited space, so I grew just a few plants of relatively many varieties. Many of the flowers I mention are also available as mixes of colours, which can give you an even bigger variety. I only grew six plants of most of the flowers; of the two largest (cleome and cosmos) I only planted two. Most of the varieties could be sown directly, but I prefer to start them in modules. This way I can get a little jumpstart on the season and I can plant out everything at the perfect spacing. Cleome and cosmos, which are tender annuals and can only be planted out after mid-May in my climate, were pre-sown at the beginning of April. The rest of the seeds I started in March and planted out in April.

All the varieties in my tiny garden are easy to grow, have no special growing requirements and will flower prolifically over a period of several months. Some of them (such as cornflower, annual clary and calendula) will even self-seed. When harvesting your flowers, you can make simple single-variety bunches, combine two or three or mix any and all into exuberant colourful bouquets. In my opinion, it is not really possible to pick a combination from the flowers below that would not be beautiful.

Pot marigold

American spider flower *(Cleome hassleriana)*

The long protruding stamens of these tall, airy flowers remind me of cat's whiskers. They have claws too – there are thorns on their stems, so be careful when you're picking them! Cleome is available in white ('Helen Campbell'), in pink ('Pink Queen'), in purple ('Violet Queen' – my favourite) and anything in between. The plants can be tricky to germinate, so make sure you have fresh seed and give them a little extra heat if you can.

Cosmos *(Cosmos bipinnatus)*

Not just the abundantly produced flowers but also the feathery foliage are a useful addition to bouquets. There are varieties in white, pink, carmine, striped, single or double, but the sweetly scented single flowered white 'Purity' remains my favourite. Cosmos is very easy to germinate and grow; just do not forget to support the plants as they get quite tall.

Sweet pea *(Lathyrus odoratus)*

Sweet peas can handle low temperatures and can be direct-sown early in spring (or even in autumn for overwintering in a greenhouse or a cold frame). But often the seeds will be eaten by hungry mice so pre-sowing inside is therefore a safer bet. Like other legumes, sweet peas send down a long root quickly and are best sown in deep pots or in rootrainers. The delicious scent is an important part of their charm and I always choose strongly scented varieties. Two of my favourites are 'Matucana' (or 'Cupani') and 'King's High Scent'. 'Matucana' is an ancient bicoloured variety in purple and magenta and 'King's High Scent' is a cream coloured modern variety with a violet picotee edge.

Pot marigold *(Calendula officinalis)*

The classic calendula colour is yellow-orange but many pretty varieties have been bred ranging from pale yellow to pink and deep orange. For my cut flower patch I chose the more subtle 'Pink Surprise' with fully double salmon-pink flowers. Calendulas are (together with sweet peas) the first of all the plants to start flowering and will attract beneficial insects into the garden too.

Pincushion flower *(Scabiosa atropurpurea)*

The little pompoms of this flower are indeed reminiscent of pincushions. Because it is actually a (short-lived) perennial, the plants grow a bit slower than others and take longer to start flowering. They compensate for it by pumping out flowers for months, well into autumn, and those flowers attract butterflies! I sowed a mix of pink and crimson colours.

Larkspur *(Consolida ajacis)*

Because this cold-tolerant annual does not like root disturbance, it is often recommended to sow the seeds directly in the garden and you can certainly do that. However, I usually treat it like all the others and pre-sow them in modules. Putting the seeds in the freezer for a week before sowing will improve germination. The flowers are best picked when a third of the blossoms on a stem are open and they are useful for adding height to arrangements. In this bed I sowed a mix of purple-blue and pink

Pincushion flower, cornflower, lupin 'Sunrise', bishop's weed, annual clary

varieties but I have grown and enjoyed others before, the most memorable being the pink and white striped 'Splish Splash'.

Cornflower (*Centaurea cyanus*)

Cornflowers start flowering early and keep going for a long time. I do not sow them in autumn because our winters are usually too cold for them to overwinter but sometimes plants will self-seed and if they do happen to survive the winter they will start flowering even earlier. Cornflowers are quite time-consuming to pick but they add a lovely 'cottage garden' vibe to bouquets. Besides, the flowers are edible and popular with bees and other pollinators. Apart from the classic blue, cornflowers are also available in white, pink and even crimson-black (variety 'Black Ball').

Bupleurum rotundifolium

Not a flower that takes the central stage but an extremely useful 'filler' for bouquets that I always wish I'd planted more of. The stems are quite sturdy and its chartreuse colour mixes well with just about anything – from pastels to more saturated darker colours.

Annual lupin (*Lupinus*)

My favourite annual lupin is 'Sunrise' with flowers that are a beautiful combination of white, gold and blue, but even better is its strong fruity scent. Lupin is probably best direct sown, but since I usually pre-sow it as the rest of my flowers, I use the deep rootrainers that I also use for sweet peas.

Bishop's weed (*Ammi visnaga*)

This is an unassuming plant with dill-like leaves and a dome of closely spaced tiny green-white flowers. A bunch of these is pretty on its own but it is also another great filler for mixed bouquets. You can also grow the more delicate bishop's flower (*Ammi majus*). As umbellifers, both will also attract beneficial insects such as hoverflies, whose larvae eat aphids.

Annual clary (*Salvia viridis*)

With this annual sage it's actually not the flowers that we grow it for but the enlarged bracts which can be white, pink or brilliant blue. These days it seems to mostly be available as a mix of colours – no matter, they are all pretty. Annual clary is easy to grow, flowers for a long time, lasts well in the vase and can even be dried.

Bouquet of cosmos, pincushion flower, annual clary and bishop's weed

TIPS FOR HARVESTING CUT FLOWERS

The best moment to pick flowers is in the early morning, because they've had all night to absorb water. All parts of the plant are then hydrated which means the cells are turgid and the stems are strong and will not flop as easily. It is also the easiest time to spot flowers that are just opening and those are generally the best to pick and will have the longest vase life. Besides, flowers that are not fully open have not been pollinated by insects yet: as soon as that happens seeds start to form and petals tend to lose their colour. If you can't pick in the morning, harvest your flowers in the evening after the temperature has dropped. In any case, do not pick in the middle of a hot summer day!

Use a sharp knife or flower snips for cutting and put your flowers straight into a bucket filled one-third with clean water. Always cut stems just above a side branch with a bud so that the plant will go on producing more flowers. Hygiene is important, so keep your tools, buckets and vases clean. Remove any leaves that would be submerged, or they'll rot. Reducing the number of leaves also reduces

Rembrandt tulip

wilting since there are fewer leaves to hydrate. Before making bouquets, leave your flowers to recover in a cool, dark spot for a few hours (or better yet: overnight).

To make your cut flowers last longer, you can add a little floral preservative to your vases, either store-bought or homemade (sugar + vinegar + bleach). Sugar will feed the flowers while the vinegar and bleach will stop bacteria from growing. But to be honest, since I can just pick a new bouquet whenever I want to, I almost never use preservatives. It does pay to refresh the water in the vase every few days though.

TIPS FOR AN EVEN LONGER CUT FLOWER SEASON

In late autumn, after the annual flowers are finished, you can still plant spring bulbs so that you'll have something to pick before the next season's annuals start flowering. Organically grown bulbs are of course best, even though you will be limited in your choice of varieties. A few of my favourite bulbs for picking are anemones (*Anemone coronaria*), scented multi-flowered daffodils like 'Bridal Crown' or 'Geranium' and elegant lily-flowered tulips such as 'White Triumphator', bright orange 'Ballerina' or deep pink 'Jacqueline'. Sometimes I also grow richly coloured striped 'Rembrandt' tulips for extravagant bouquets. But any tulip that has a long enough stem is good for cutting and will find its admirers.

Our current vegetable garden

I had my very first vegetable garden when I was 12 years old. In spring, my parents bought a lot of seed packets for their own garden and I was mesmerised by the colourful images on the packets and excited by the idea that I too could actually grow something to eat. I approached gardening seriously, carefully studied the information on the back of the packets and even made a planting plan. But in order to fit everything in, including large plants like celeriac and cabbage onto my meagre two square metres, I sowed the vegetables a little closer together. To my dismay, all I ended up harvesting were some measly radishes and prematurely bolting lettuce. I threw in the towel and resigned myself to helping my parents in their kitchen garden where everything grew marvellously. What I did not know then was that my tiny plot was an endeavour bound to fail no matter how well I cared for my little garden, due to it being sited right under a huge acacia tree that not only cast a lot of shade but also withdrew water and nutrients. My parents' garden flourished because it was in full sun on beautiful loamy soil. I've gardened on many different plots since, each garden benefiting from the experiences I gained from the previous ones. Whenever I start a new garden, my goal is to leave the soil in a better shape than it was when I started – increasing the organic matter content and encouraging abundant soil life through permaculture gardening methods.

Apart from being active in our community garden, since 2003 we have also rented a plot on an organic allotment about 5km (3 miles) from our house. Founded in the late 60s, it is the oldest organic allotment garden in the Netherlands. Our first plot was 120m² (1300ft²) and we soon outgrew it. In the following years we kept adding plot after plot, and at the peak moment, we were cultivating almost 400m² (4300ft²) of annual vegetables, fruit trees, bushes and flowers. Unfortunately, there came a moment when we had to give up our plot because the owner no longer wanted to rent it out to the allotment association. We lost fruit trees that were too big to transplant and started dreaming of a plot that would be truly ours and would allow for developing a more permanent garden.

This dream came true in 2015 when we were able to buy our current plot (a stone's throw away from the plots we had rented), which is 966m² (almost ¼ acre) in total. I spent the fall of 2015 making a design and in January 2016 we started turning it into a reality.

Most of the plot is being developed into an edible forest and planted with a combination of nut and fruit trees, bushes and perennial vegetables and herbs. Our kitchen garden (the part of the plot where we grow annual vegetables) occupies less than a sixth of the total area.

From south to north, the design of the plot moves from elements requiring regular work and attention such as the raised beds with annual vegetables and our greenhouse, to trees and shrubs that can get by with just occasional pruning and mulching. Because the southern part of the garden was mostly free from perennial weeds when we took over, no clearance mulch was necessary and we could install our raised beds right away. There are 12 large raised beds (1.2 x 2.8-3m / 4 x 9-10ft) and four small ones, edged with Douglas pine. Under the hazel in the middle of the plot we found a huge neglected compost heap where organic waste had probably been deposited for years. After we removed the nettles growing on top, there was a lot of well-rotted compost that we could use to fill our raised beds. To ensure a reliable water supply, we had a well and pump installed close to the kitchen garden since that is the only area that needs to be watered regularly. Apart from that we're also collecting rainwater from the roof of our little shed and from the roof of the greenhouse.

To the left of the raised beds is our three-compartment-composting installation and an approximately three metre wide strip with three pear trees on dwarfing rootstock. The trees are underplanted with a mix of herbs and flowers that attract pollinators and other beneficial insects. The flowering starts with spring bulbs, such as snowdrops and daffodils, and the early flowering perennial leopard's bane (*Doronicum orientale*). Later there are lupins, foxgloves, lemon balm, calendula, wild oregano and evening primrose.

Pears underplanted with a mix of herbs and flowers that attract beneficial insects

My permaculture cottage garden

Pond construction

To the right of the kitchen garden is what I call my 'permaculture cottage garden': an informal mix of perennial plants and (self-sowing) annuals. I wanted this part of the garden to be colourful and pretty as well as productive, so I aimed to include mainly plants that have an ornamental value as well as some edible parts and mixed those with lots of flowers. There are fruit trees (cherry 'Kordia' and red-fleshed apple 'Calypso'), fruiting bushes (gooseberries, honeyberries and Nanking cherry), herbs (fennel, chives, lovage, mint), annual and perennial vegetables and edible flowers (chard, artichokes, calendula, borage). These are interplanted with flowers, most of which can be cut for the vase, such as peonies, delphinium, *Veronica longifolia* and New England asters. This is also the part of the garden housing our greenhouse. In summer the glass greenhouse is full of warm-loving crops: tomatoes of course, but also aubergines, basil, peppers, melons and sweet potatoes. In winter we plant it with cold-resistant crops such as mustards, hardy lettuces and spinach, peas for pea shoots and spring onions. I also like to tuck in some flowers for early bouquets. Anemones (*Anemone coronaria*) can be planted in late fall (after we harvest our sweet potatoes), will overwinter happily and start pumping lots of flowers as soon as temperatures rise and the days get a little longer.

The pond attracts slug-eating frogs and toads

To the north of the kitchen garden we made a little pond. As any element in a good permaculture design, it fulfils several functions: it grows edible aquatic plants such as common spatterdock (*Nuphar lutea*), water fringe (*Nypmhoides peltata*) and arrowhead (*Sagittaria sagittifolia*), and the body of water moderates temperatures, accumulating warmth during the day and slowly releasing it through the night, protecting the neighbouring peach and apricot from spring frosts. But most importantly, it attracts a lot of wildlife, including slug-eating frogs and toads.

The question I probably get asked most often is how much time the garden 'costs', the assumption often being that it is pretty much a full-time job. I do not feel like it 'costs' me anything because the hours I spend in the garden are often some of the happiest and most peaceful of my week. But I do understand that people like to know how much time is involved in tending a relatively large and diverse plot like ours. Well, most of the gardening is done by me and my husband and since we both work full time, the time we can spend in the garden is limited to one or two evenings during the week and the weekends. We do get occasional help from friends and family with bigger jobs like digging the pond or building the greenhouse. Because the majority of the plot is planted with perennial plants, most of the time is spent taking care of the kitchen garden where annuals are grown. I find that the key to keeping the garden low maintenance is doing the important jobs in time, most importantly applying a layer of mulch at the beginning of the season. This saves us countless hours of weeding, hoeing and watering later on!

I feel deeply thankful for this plot that we get to tend and which not only feeds us but also gives me the opportunity to experiment with new ideas. What I learn gardening here inspires my work as a garden writer and designer and hopefully benefits my readers and clients too.

CHAPTER 10

Permaculture Kitchen Garden throughout the Year

In this overview I share what we do in the garden each month: what we sow (both undercover and outside in the garden), what we harvest and what other important jobs there are to take care of. Your climate might be a little different from ours and you might need to adapt the sowing and planting dates because of that, but I hope this overview will provide you with a guideline.

JANUARY

Personally, I consider the month of January a time-out from active gardening. We do of course still visit our plot to harvest hardy crops, but, especially when the ground is covered in snow, there is little to do other than prune our fruit trees and bushes. No crops can be planted and our windowsill does not get enough light yet to make sowing inside worthwhile. Therefore January is above all a month for planning this year's growing season, perusing seed catalogues and both literally and figuratively sharpening the tools.

Thompson & Morgan
LETTUCE
Stryker
VEGETABLE
LARGER AND TALLER HEARTED 'ROMAINE'
doorlevende spinazie
beta vulgaris
Selectie van snijbiet met smallere stengels en donkergroen blad. Sterke groeikracht, heel de zomer klaar om te snijden en te hergroeien, goede winterhardheid. Afdekken met bladeren of stro bij strenge vorst.
verwijderen. Mooie kleine oogst in
Zaaien april tot augustus.Tweejarig
gronden.
Thompson & Morgan
TOMATO
Matina
CROPS WELL OUTDOORS
Pastinaak
Pastinaak is een oude wort
Ter plaatse zaaien
Voorkeur voo
Biologisch geteelde groentezaden
819B
Boerenkool
Prijsgroep
2
menas
nde Zwarte

DRAWING A PLAN

If this is going to be your first garden season or if you are starting in a new spot, this is the time to plan the layout of your kitchen garden. Make a drawing to scale, including any important permanent features such as a shed, trees or water source. Consider any elements that might cast shadow over the garden (buildings, trees). Then decide on the size and orientation of your beds and the width of your paths. You may even want to take your plan to the garden and use canes and string to map out the layout in 3D to see how it feels; are the beds too wide or the paths too narrow? Since constructing the beds will hopefully be a one-time job, it pays to think through your layout carefully.

PLANNING THE CROPS

I usually consult my family about anything they would like me to grow, make a list and then try to fit all that I'm planning to grow into the garden plan. Some beds will be planted as a polyculture, but some crops are assigned their own bed for the sake of practicality. This is, for example, the case for early potatoes: growing them all in one bed means I can easily use row covers to protect them from late frosts. Per bed, I'll usually plan at least two plantings that can follow each other in the course of the season. Even though the plan will likely get tweaked and adjusted later on, it is nevertheless helpful to have one to start with.

TESTING VIABILITY OF OLD SEEDS

The life span of seeds varies greatly depending on the crop and the way they were stored. If you do not want to waste time and compost on seeds that may never germinate, you can test the germination rate of older seeds before sowing them. To do this, put about 20 seeds on a piece of moist kitchen towel. Put it in a plastic or glass container that you can seal. Label the container with the date and name of the variety. Leave the container at room temperature and start checking for germination daily from three days onwards. Keep the kitchen towel moist with a spray bottle and keep track of how many seeds (if any) germinate. Most crops will germinate within a week, but some (such as parsnips) can take more than three. The age of the seeds not only influences the germination rate but also the speed at which the seeds will germinate – the older the seeds, the longer they take. Lastly, keep in mind that a polyculture is a good way to use up old seeds with uncertain germination rate.

HARVESTING Leeks, parsnips, Jerusalem artichokes, Brussels sprouts, kale, chard, winter purslane, corn salad, mustard greens, radicchio.

FEBRUARY

Even though February can still be very cold, there are also often days that allow for some serious outside work. Weather permitting, you can start constructing your beds and filling them with compost. This is also the month when I sort out my pots, prepare a potting mix for sowing and start the first seeds on our sunny windowsill.

POTTING MIX

In February I buy any materials I need for creating my own potting mix. For the past few years, this is the mix I have been using for starting most of my seeds: 5 parts cocopeat, 4 parts vermiculite or perlite and 1-3 parts homemade sifted compost from our wormery (vermicompost). The mix is peat-free and works well for almost anything. The cocopeat holds moisture, the perlite or vermiculite aerates it and allows for good drainage and optimum root development, while the vermicompost supplies the necessary nutrients. The lower amount of compost is sufficient for starting seeds that will later be potted on. The higher amount is better for plants such as corn that grow in the same pots until they're planted out and I also use it when potting on seedlings such as tomatoes and peppers. I prepare a fair amount of the mix at the same time and store it in a large bin next to my potting bench in order to have it ready whenever I want to start a crop inside.

SOWING AUBERGINES AND PEPPERS

These two heat-loving crops need a relatively long growing season, which means we need to start them early. They both also need quite high temperatures to germinate (preferably above 20°C/68°F). At this time of year our house is colder than that, so I start the seeds in a small heated propagator. When the seedlings are big enough for pricking out, I plant them into 5cm pots with a richer potting mix and move them into a propagator that is not heated. After they fill the pots I repot them again into 9cm pots by which time they do not need the protection of a propagator. Both aubergines and peppers will require heat throughout their life and if you don't have a greenhouse, the keys to success in our climate are choosing the right varieties and planting them in a warm and sunny spot. Outside, I've had the best results with aubergine 'Early Black Egg' and 'Morden Midget'. Aubergines also grow well in pots on a sunny balcony or a patio for which compact varieties such as 'White Egg' or 'Little Fingers' are especially suitable.

BROAD BEANS AND PEAS

Broad beans and peas are on the opposite side of the spectrum: they germinate even in quite low temperatures and are considerably hardy. In climates with relatively mild winters, this makes them suitable for sowing in late autumn. In our climate, autumn sowing is a gamble, one that I do not really consider worthwhile because we often lose most, if not all of the plants to a cold spell and even if we don't, the harvest will not be that much earlier than from this year's early under-cover sowing. I like to pre-sprout the seeds, by soaking them in water overnight and then keeping them moist until they start sprouting. This way only sprouted seeds are sown which prevents me from wasting potting mix and precious windowsill space on seeds that might not be viable. I like to sow both broad beans and peas in rootrainers that allow for optimum root development.

SOWING INSIDE Sweet and hot peppers, aubergine, broad beans, peas, sugar snap peas and snow peas, lettuce, spinach.

HARVESTING Leeks, parsnips, Jerusalem artichokes, Brussels sprouts, kale, chard, winter purslane, corn salad, land cress, mustard greens.

MARCH

The days are getting noticeably longer and the soil is slowly warming up which means the first hardy vegetables can usually be direct-sown in the garden, if necessary under the protection of a row cover. Meanwhile inside, we are continuing to start more and more crops on the windowsill and we're sprouting early potatoes to plant in the second half of the month.

CLEARANCE MULCH

Even though you can apply clearance mulch pretty much any time, in our climate, my preferred time to do so is in March. This is before the weeds really take off, but after the soil is (usually) no longer stone cold. February or April is usually also fine but try not to leave it much later. If you wait too long (and sometimes that happens here too because we do not get to it in time) and the weeds have already put on substantial growth, covering them for the rest of the season might not be enough to kill them. When we are going to clear a patch, we go to a bicycle store and ask if we can have some of the large pieces of cardboard the bicycles are packed in. We remove all tape and staples and lay the cardboard down with generous overlap and weigh it down with bricks and tiles. If you want to obscure the cardboard, either top it with a substantial layer of weed-free material such as mushroom compost, and/or start winter and summer squash plants in April to plant through holes in the cardboard.

DIRECT-SOWING

There are many reasons for starting plants under cover: you can control the circumstances such as moisture and temperature, which leads to better germination. In the garden, sturdy plants are less susceptible to slug damage than tiny seedlings that have just emerged. You can set the plants out at optimum spacing and make better use of the available space. However, there are some crops that are better suited to direct-sowing in the garden, mainly root vegetables such as carrots and parsnips which do not like to be transplanted and whose roots would suffer if sown in relatively shallow pots. When sowing directly, it is best to wait until the soil has warmed up a bit – no need to know the exact temperature, just feel on your forearm whether it is still cold to the touch or not. In cold and wet soil, seeds will sooner rot than germinate, so it's always better to practise patience and wait till the circumstances are right. If you want to speed things up, you can also use row covers to make the soil warm up faster before sowing.

CHITTING AND PLANTING EARLY POTATOES

Especially if your garden is quite small, trying to grow all the potatoes you eat is probably not the best use of the space. But I always try to plant at least a few early potatoes, because those, unlike regular maincrop potatoes, are a true treat. Since they are harvested early, they allow for a follow-up crop too. There is some debate on whether 'chitting' (letting the tubers sprout indoors prior to planting) actually makes that much of a difference, but it seems worthwhile to me, at least in early potatoes. To do so, I put the potatoes in egg cartons, with the side with the most 'eyes' facing up. I leave the trays in a cool, light spot away from direct sunlight (which to be truthful is the windowsill in my son's bedroom and he is not terribly thrilled about that). I plant the potatoes when the soil has warmed up a bit and protect them with a row cover.

SOWING INSIDE Sweet and hot peppers, aubergine, tomatoes, basil, broad beans, peas, sugar snap peas and snow peas, lettuce, artichokes, kale, beetroot, broccoli, kohlrabi, celery, celeriac.

SOWING OUTSIDE Broad beans, peas, radishes, mustard greens, rocket, spring onions, lettuce, parsnips, carrots, turnips, parsley, spinach, leeks, orache.

PLANTING Early potatoes, garlic, onion sets.

HARVESTING Kale, leeks, winter purslane, mustard greens, corn salad, parsnips, Jerusalem artichokes, Brussels sprouts, chard.

APRIL

April is a busy sowing month, both outside in the garden and under cover. The weather can still change fast and often, but on the whole, the soil is warm enough to start many crops outside as well as plant out hardy crops that were started undercover earlier. Between clearing the last of the overwintered vegetables and planting spring crops, this is a good opportunity to spread an annual dose of (homemade) compost or well-rotted manure on all our beds.

SPREADING COMPOST

All our beds get a top dressing of about two wheelbarrows of compost or well-rotted manure every spring. This could be done in autumn as well, but since in autumn most of the beds are still full of hardy crops, spreading compost around and between the plants would be cumbersome. We prefer to wait till spring, after the winter crops are finished and cleared and before spring crops have been sown or planted. For beds in which I will be planting, I usually do not bother with sifting the compost, but if I want to sow directly, I will remove any larger pieces of plant material that have not decomposed properly and throw them on a new compost pile. After the compartments of our composting installation have been emptied, we fill them up again and cover the top with a piece of cardboard, so that a winter squash can be planted in each later.

SWEET POTATO SLIPS

For the past few years I've been growing sweet potatoes in my garden – either in a sheltered spot outside, or in the greenhouse where they get the heat these (sub) tropical plants require in order to give us a decent harvest. The first year I bought organic plants of a variety that is suited to our climate (it's called 'Indosweet' but more and more varieties are becoming available). In the following years I kept a few of our best tubers till spring and used those to start my own plants. For this, I cut the tubers in half and put them in a shallow container filled with water. In my experience, the warmer the spot, the faster they will sprout, so I often put them in my heated propagator. When the shoots appear, I break them off and let them root in a glass of water before potting them on. I usually wait to plant out until the weather is reliably warm, the end of May/ beginning of June.

POTTING ON AND MOVING OUT

In spring, the situation on our windowsills resembles a carefully orchestrated dance – only windowsills facing south receive sufficient light for starting seedlings, which is why I try to use the available space as efficiently as possible. As soon as any space becomes available because a crop has been planted out, new seed trays and pots will fill it. Tomatoes, peppers and aubergines that have been sown earlier need the sheltered environment for a bit longer and are potted on when they have filled their pots. Any plants that look like they could use a little extra are fed the diluted liquid from our wormery.

SOWING INSIDE Winter and summer squashes, cucumber, tomatoes, melons, basil, beans, cauliflower, celery, celeriac, nasturtiums, kale, sweet corn, cabbages, broccoli.

SOWING OUTSIDE Beetroot, carrots, spring onions, peas, mustard greens, radishes, leeks, kales, orache, parsley, chard, lettuce.

HARVESTING The last of the overwintered kale, leeks, winter purslane, mustard greens, corn salad, parsnips and chard, new season's asparagus, rhubarb, mustard greens, rocket, spinach and perennial herbs.

MAY

By May the gardening season is in full swing and after planting out tender vegetables in the second half of the month, all of our beds are full. This also means that some pests might start emerging and susceptible crops such as cabbages and carrots will benefit from the protection of insect netting. Mulch applied now will save tons of work later.

THINNING

Plants that are crowded will be competing for light, water and nutrients and grow poorly as a result. It does not matter whether your seedlings are crowded because of weeds or because you sowed the seeds too closely; to get a good crop, it is important to give your plants sufficient breathing space. This means not only removing any weeds that emerge but also thinning the crop you sowed early on. Luckily, nothing needs to be wasted – if you're careful, you can often replant some of your seedlings elsewhere. And if you do not need more plants, you can usually eat the thinnings. One crop that I thin extra carefully is carrots, because the scent of the plants might attract the dreaded carrot fly. It is best to thin carrots in the evening or in still conditions and bury the thinnings in the compost heap (if you're not going to eat them).

PROTECTING CROPS FROM PESTS

We try to make sure our soil is as healthy as possible, so that the plants grown in it will be healthy and capable of withstanding the occasional appearance of pests to which no garden is immune.

We also include plants in our garden that attract natural predators: for example, sweet cicely and fennel are a magnet for hoverflies whose larvae feed on aphids.

For crops that are especially susceptible, we sometimes resort to creating a physical barrier. In early spring, a row cover will not only provide a little extra warmth, but, for example, will also protect our mustard greens against pigeons. Later, it can protect newly planted kales and cabbages (to which several species of butterfly are very partial). Apart from this we also net our strawberries, currants and gooseberries to keep birds from eating them.

HARDENING OFF TENDER VEGETABLES

After mid-May it is usually safe to plant out tender vegetables such as courgettes and tomatoes. To soften the transition from the sheltered environment inside, I let them get used to the harsher circumstances outside gradually. At least a week prior to planting out, I start taking them to a sheltered spot in our backyard, for a couple of hours at a time, when the weather is warm. Their stay outside is gradually prolonged, but I put them in the shed at night, until they are used to the stronger light, temperature fluctuations and movement of air outside and can be planted out without risking a temporary growth stop. Alternatively, if hardening off is not practical in your circumstances, you might use small cloches to protect individual plants for the first week or two after planting out, or a row cover to protect a whole bed at the same time.

SOWING INSIDE Winter and summer squashes, cucumbers, sweet corn, cauliflower, kale.

SOWING OUTSIDE Beans, sweet corn, chard, broccoli, courgette, beetroot, carrots, kale, lettuce, cabbages.

HARVESTING Asparagus, rhubarb, radishes, mustard greens, rocket, lettuce, spinach, annual and perennial herbs.

JUNE

June is the month of the summer solstice, which, even though it is the official beginning of summer, is also a turning point after which the days start getting shorter again. For the gardener, it is a signal to stop harvesting rhubarb and asparagus and start sowing certain day-length sensitive crops. We also like to mark this point in the year with a proper midsummer celebration.

MIDSUMMER

The longest day which falls around 21st June is the beginning of the astronomical summer. We usually try to take this opportunity to pause for a bit and celebrate the beauty and abundance of the garden by inviting a few friends over for a little garden party. I fill vases with lavish bouquets and make appetisers with edible flowers and little cakes with berries. But midsummer is also a point in the year when we stop harvesting perennial crops like rhubarb and asparagus and let them build up energy for next year. On the other hand, there are some day-length sensitive crops that are best started after the days begin to shorten. If you sow vegetables like fennel and pak choi before midsummer, they will likely bolt before they have made a worthwhile crop.

DRYING HERBS

Around the longest day is a good time to harvest herbs for drying because at this moment they are full of aromatic oils and both their taste and their medicinal properties are at their peak. To be able to enjoy a homegrown tisane during the winter too, I cut huge bunches of my favourite tea herbs in June: lemon balm, different varieties of mint and lemon verbena. Other herbs I harvest mainly for medicinal teas such as sage to fight sore throats. The best time to cut herbs for drying is on a sunny day before noon, after the dew has dried up. I bind the bunches together with a twine and hang them in our living room, away from direct sunlight. When the leaves are completely dry, I strip them off the stalks and store them in glass jars. I like to add some dried flowers to my teas too: lavender, chamomile, the petals of calendula and scented roses. These I dry in a single layer on a piece of newspaper.

RADICCHIO

Though radicchio (a red form of chicory) is slowly gaining a following in northern Europe, it is nowhere near as popular here as it is in Italy, where it is lovingly called *'il fiore che si mangia'* – 'the flower that you eat'. I've come to appreciate the bitter, cleansing taste of this beautiful crop as much as I like its cousins endive and witloof, which are, together with kale and beetroot, the quintessential vegetables of the Dutch cuisine. Because radicchio is quite hardy, it is a very useful crop for late autumn and early winter. The bitter taste makes it virtually immune to pest problems and its deep root makes it fairly resistant to dry conditions. However, if you're aiming for nice dense hearts, the timing can be a little tricky. I have had the most success with sowing around midsummer, in rows about 25-30cm (10-12in) apart. I like both the tall 'di Treviso' type of chicory as well as the more rounded heads of 'di Chioggia'.

SOWING OUTSIDE Fennel, beetroot, carrots, beans, chicories, endive, Oriental brassicas, courgette, cucumber, sweet corn, chard, spring onions.

HARVESTING Asparagus and rhubarb (till midsummer), beetroot, broad beans, peas, radishes, lettuce, courgette, chard, carrots, mustard greens, kohlrabi, earliest potatoes, turnips.

JULY

In July the garden begins to reach the height of its productivity and it is important to stay on top of things: water when the soil gets too dry, apply liquid feed to hungry crops and above all, keep harvesting (especially fruiting vegetables such as courgettes) so that the plants keep producing. Whenever a crop is cleared, we take the opportunity to sow or plant a new one. Towards the end of this month we usually leave for our three week holiday and before we go, I try to check off all the items on my 'pre-holiday to-do list'.

SECOND CROPS

By July, many early crops are finished which means an opportunity to re-sow or replant to keep the harvests coming well into the winter. To prevent disease and pest problems, it's better not to follow a crop with another one from the same botanical family. In some cases, an unrelated crop can even have a distinctly beneficial impact on the following one: leeks after broad beans benefit from the nitrogen left in the soil, kale after garlic benefits from the antifungal properties of the preceding crop. After lifting early potatoes, I like to plant courgettes for a late crop. Peas and sugar snap require some support to climb up against so it makes sense to follow them with cucumbers and gherkins which also grow well vertically.

HARVESTING GARLIC

When it comes to harvesting onions, you can wait till the leaves are almost completely dry and lying down, but for garlic, it's better to harvest earlier, when some of the leaves are still green. Autumn-planted garlic should be ready for harvest around the end of June/beginning of July. Should you wait too long, the cloves of the bulb might start to separate and sprout, which would make it unsuitable for storage. After harvest, let the bulbs dry in a dry, breezy spot – I hang them under a shed overhang. When dry, garlic can be gathered into decorative plaits (or simple bunches) and hung in a cool place – the optimum storage temperature is between 5-10°C (40-50°F). Depending on the variety and storage conditions, garlic will keep for up to 12 months.

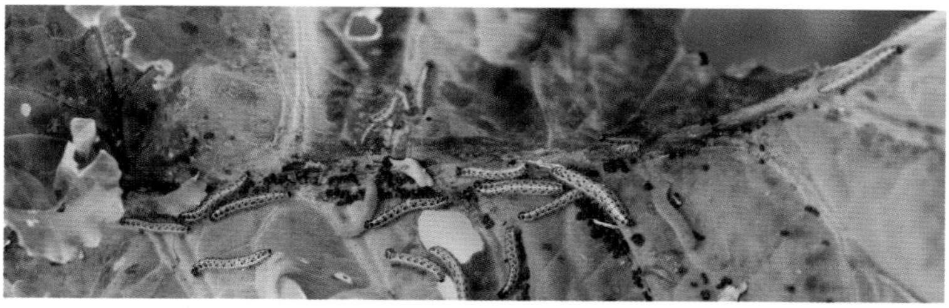

PRE-HOLIDAY TO-DO LIST

If we did not have school-going children, I would definitely not choose to go on holiday in the middle of summer when my garden is at its most beautiful and most productive. But because we leave our garden for a few weeks every summer in order to visit my family in the Czech Republic, I've compiled a little to-do list of jobs to accomplish before we go on holiday:

1. Remove all weeds – in the warm summer weather, even the tiniest ones can grow into monstrous proportions in no time
2. Replenish the layer of mulch if needed
3. Check plants for pests (such as the yellow eggs of the cabbage butterflies on the underside of kale leaves) and remove any diseased plants
4. Apply liquid feed to hungry crops such as cabbages and courgettes if necessary
5. Make sure the soil is thoroughly moist before we leave
6. Find a friend or family member willing to water the greenhouse once a week in exchange for sun-ripened tomatoes

SOWING OUTSIDE Carrots, beetroot, bush beans, chard, Oriental brassicas (pak choi, tatsoi), spring onions, fennel, chicory, endive, Oriental radishes, chard, kale, kohlrabi.

HARVESTING Lettuce, beetroot, carrots, turnips, kohlrabi, broccoli, spring onions, early potatoes, courgette, tomatoes, garlic, annual and perennial herbs.

AUGUST

We usually spend the first two weeks of August at my parents' house in the Czech Republic, but since they too have a large garden full of edibles, it in no way means that I take a break from gardening. Together with my mother we make fruit preserves, dry wild mushrooms for the winter and ferment gherkins. And when we get back to the Netherlands, more harvesting awaits us, including the first sweet corn.

SOWING ORIENTAL RADISHES

Even though radishes are one of my favourite spring vegetables, they are becoming a bit of a gamble due to the weather turning more and more unpredictable; in a dry hot spring radishes might bolt before we get any harvest to speak of. Compared to that, Oriental radishes sown in July or August are more of a sure thing and can often be harvested well into autumn or even winter. Because they are generally much larger than classic spring radishes, I sow them further apart, in rows spaced 20cm (8in). In the warm soil they germinate quickly and I thin them for the first time about three weeks later. The young leaves are nice in stir fries or stirred into mashed potatoes (something the Dutch do with many vegetables). About five weeks after sowing, I can pick the first smallish roots which gives the remaining plants space to develop into large roots. There are quite a few different types and varieties available, but some of my favourites are 'Shunkyo' (pink on the outside with white flesh inside) and 'Green Meat' (long white roots which are green tinted inside and are very juicy and sweet).

PRESERVING THE ABUNDANCE/ LACTOFERMENTATION

As I mentioned before, my aim is to have a continuous supply of fresh vegetables from the garden. We do make chutneys to eat with curry (a regular menu item in our household) and some fruit jams and jellies but otherwise we do little traditional canning. However, I do enjoy experimenting with lactofermentation, since unlike most other preserving methods, it actually increases the nutritional value of the vegetables. My favourite vegetable for quick fermentation is gherkins and here's a simple way to preserve them:

Fill a large glass jar (at least 2 litre/2qt capacity) with gherkins, tucking a few dill fronds and garlic cloves between the layers. Make a brine by dissolving 30g (1oz) of salt per litre of water. Pour the brine over the gherkins and put a weight on top of them so that they remain submerged. Leave the gherkins in a warm place for about three to five days (or longer if you prefer a more sour taste). The fermented gherkins keep for several weeks in the fridge.

HARVESTING SWEET CORN

There are few vegetables in which freshness determines the taste to the same extent as in sweet corn, but the moment of harvest is important too: if you pick too early the taste has not yet fully developed, if you pick too late it will be starchy rather than sweet. I try to plan my crop so that the first corn can be harvested when we come home from our summer holiday. The corn is usually ready when the silks turn brown, but to be sure I gently pull back a few leaves and press a kernel with my fingernail. If the juice that comes out is watery, it is not ready yet – it should be milky white.

To enjoy heirloom sweet corn at its best, the advice is to have the water boiling before you pick your corn. We sometimes feast on sweet corn boiled briefly on a little camping stove right in the garden. If you don't want to turn eating sweet corn into a race, you might be better off growing one of the 'supersweet' or 'tendersweet' varieties in which the conversion of sugar to starch is much slower.

SOWING OUTSIDE Oriental radishes, rocket, mustard greens, corn salad, winter purslane, leaf endive, land cress, Oriental brassicas, hardy lettuce.

HARVESTING Courgettes, tomatoes, peppers, aubergine, tomatillos, gherkins, cucumbers, lettuce, beetroot, carrots, spring onions, chard, potatoes, garlic, beans, sweet corn, broccoli, annual and perennial herbs.

SEPTEMBER

September is a month to savour: as summer slowly turns into autumn the weather is often still very beautiful, but the pressure is off. We dig up the last potatoes and store them in the cellar and keep our eyes open for signs of late blight in tomatoes, so that we can remove diseased plants as soon as possible. As the days shorten, we make sowings of hardy greens in the cold frame or the greenhouse for picking throughout the winter.

HARVESTING POTATOES

Most of the potatoes we grow are for immediate consumption and we lift them as and when we want to eat them. But by the end of September, when the plants start to die down, we harvest anything that is left to store in our little cellar. On a dry, sunny day, I lift the remaining potatoes with a fork, careful not to stab them. Then I leave them on the surface of the soil to dry for about two hours, after which they can be stored. I store my potatoes in a single layer in crates that can be stacked on top of each other and cover them with newspaper to protect them from light. Heavy-duty paper or hessian sacks are a good solution too, but there is more risk of one rotting potato infecting others. The optimum temperature for storing potatoes is between 4-10°C (40-50°F).

DEALING WITH BLIGHT IN TOMATOES

With maybe the exception of a few (partially) resistant varieties, sooner or later, most tomatoes grown outside in our rainy climate are bound to get infected with late blight (*Phytophtora infestans*). In an especially rainy summer, even the blight-tolerant varieties I stick to for outdoor growing might start displaying the brown spots on their leaves by September. If only the odd leaf is infected, I start by removing those, but if the infection is more severe, it is better to remove the whole plants as quickly as possible. The disease spores do not survive on dead plant material, which means most of the plant can be composted. I do not like to add the fruits to the compost heap though, because the spores might survive on the seeds and the disease might be perpetuated with volunteer tomato plants the next year.

IMPACT OF DAYLIGHT LENGTH

The growth of most crops slows down considerably when day length drops below 10 hours, and even greens such as spinach, mustard and winter purslane, which are less affected, need to have a well-established root system before the days become too short. At our 52nd parallel, the date after which days become shorter than 10 hours, is 26th October. From experience I know that greens for cut-and-come-again winter picking from the cold frame should be sown about six weeks prior to that date. For individual plants of, for example, mibuna, mizuna and hardy romaine lettuces, which will be harvested 'leaf-by-leaf', I aim to sow at the very beginning of September. Hearting hardy lettuces such as 'Kweik' and endive are best sown a week or two before that.

SOWING UNDER COVER Corn salad, rocket, mustard greens, leaf endive, pak choi, mibuna, mizuna.

HARVESTING Tomatoes, aubergines, peppers, tomatillos, sweet corn, courgettes, gherkins, cucumbers, melons, lettuce, beetroot, carrots, fennel, beans, Oriental cabbages, Oriental radishes.

OCTOBER

If we're lucky, October will still bring some sunny days for our winter squash to ripen fully on the vine and for beans to dry on the plants. But if the weather turns cold and wet, we'll bring them inside to cure and to dry properly before storing them. We'll also start planting spring bulbs both in containers and outside in the garden.

HARVESTING AND STORING WINTER SQUASH

For best taste, winter squash fruits should be left on the plant until they are completely ripe. It is a good idea to remove any leaves that might be shading the fruits towards the end of the season, so that they get maximum sun exposure. Usually the stalk turning dry and 'cracking' is a sign that the fruit is ripe. When picking the fruits, cut them off with a long piece of the stem attached but resist carrying the fruit by its stem because if it breaks off, the wound would be open to rot. To ensure a long storage life the fruits need to be 'cured' after harvesting. This means leaving them in a sunny warm spot for about a week or two to toughen their skin. We leave them prettily arranged on a south-facing windowsill in our living room where they double as fall décor. The optimum temperature for storing winter squash is 10-15°C (50-60°F) – in our case, in crates under the bed in our unheated bedroom.

PLANTING SPRING BULBS

Even though spring bulbs are not edible (with the exception of tulip petals), there are good reasons to add some to your garden. For one, they occupy the ground mostly during the 'off-season': you can plant them as late as December (though October is better) and they are finished before tender vegetables can be planted out. Growing them is as easy as making a hole in the ground and putting a bulb in (preferably the right side up) and especially the early flowering ones such as crocuses are also an important source of nectar for pollinators. Apart from planting bulbs in the garden, I always plant a bulb lasagne in our zinc tub as well as more bulbs in containers to be placed close to our back door in spring. Organically grown bulbs are of course best, but you will be quite limited in your choice. However, I am of the 'more is better than rare' school of thought when it comes to bulbs. I prefer to have a mass of the most common of daffodils in my garden than a few rarities that will make little impact. I also grow some daffodils and tulips for cutting in my vegetable beds. If planted a little deeper than usual, they can stay in place and a summer crop can be planted over the bulbs after the leaves have died down.

DRYING BEANS AND CORN

If the weather is dry and sunny, we will leave any beans and corn we want to store for winter on the plants as long as possible. If we're lucky, they might dry completely on the plant; if not, we will need to continue drying them inside. To do so we shell the beans and dry them in a single layer before putting them in glass jars. Corn kernels can only be removed from the cob when they are sufficiently dry, so if the weather is turning wet or if birds are threatening our harvest, we'll bring the corn inside and hang the ears upside down in the living room. While we keep some beans for planting the next spring, we do not do this with corn which is wind pollinated and prone to inbreeding. A population of 200 corn plants is recommended for seed saving and even if we had enough space to grow that many, it would be difficult to protect them from cross-pollination.

HARVESTING
Winter squash, carrots, beetroot, kale, Oriental brassicas, fennel, chard, lettuce, beans and corn for drying.

PLANTING Garlic, shallots, spring bulbs.

NOVEMBER

November is the month when we often experience the first frost, one of the moments that divides the gardening year into a 'before' and an 'after'. While frost brings about the definitive end of any frost-tender vegetables that were hanging by a thread, it also brings other, hardy crops into the spotlight by making them taste sweeter. The first frost is also a sign to dig up our yacon, put the panes back on the cold frame and protect moderately hardy crops with a row cover.

PLANTING GARLIC

There are two types of garlic: softneck and hardneck. In softneck (*Allium sativum*), each bulb consists of a circle of large cloves on the outside with one or two rows of small cloves inside. Hardneck (*Allium sativum* var. *ophioscordum*) produces fewer cloves but they tend to be larger. While softneck can be planted both in autumn and in early spring, hardneck is only suited to autumn planting. In order to produce a large bulb, this type of garlic needs at least a month of temperatures below 10°C (50°F). For planting, I choose the largest cloves from each bulb and space them about 20cm (8in) apart, in both directions. The remaining smaller cloves can be planted closer together and harvested early as green garlic. Garlic prefers light, fertile, well-draining soil – growing it in raised beds amended with plenty of compost works well for us.

SWEETER AFTER A FROST

Because frost is damaging to plant cells, some vegetables developed a clever way to lower its impact. Certain vegetables react to cooler temperatures by converting some of their stored starch into soluble sugar and releasing that into their internal circulation. This has a similar effect to adding an antifreeze to a windshield washer fluid: it lowers the freezing point and thereby protects the plant cells from damage in sub-zero temperatures. It is a smart mechanism by which the plant protects itself – the sweet taste is only a pleasant side-effect for the eater. The effect is noticeable both in leafy vegetables such as kale or Brussels sprouts and in root vegetables such as parsnips, carrots and celeriac.

HARVESTING AND STORING YACON

Just like with dahlias (which by the way are edible too), the nutritious tubers of yacon (*Smallanthus sonchifolius*) are best dug up after the first light frost. Unlike Jerusalem artichokes, which can be left in the ground and harvested throughout the winter as needed, yacon tubers are best stored in a frost-free cellar. Crunchiness and juiciness are a big part of their charm and in order to keep them from drying out, we store them in layers of sand in large buckets. The plants can be extremely productive – one of ours yielded 6kg (13lb) last year. Apart from the large tubers, each plant also produces smaller knobbly ones closer to the soil surface – these are the ones to save for planting next spring.

PLANTING Garlic and shallots, spring bulbs.

HARVESTING Kale, leeks, Brussels sprouts, parsnips, chard, Jerusalem artichokes, yacon, Oriental brassicas, radicchio, endive, red and green cabbage, parsley, Oriental radishes, sweet potatoes.

DECEMBER

In December the days get progressively shorter until we reach the winter solstice. It is the month when we 'put the garden to bed' for the winter, covering any empty beds with a blanket of leaves or straw. We look back and reflect on the successes and failures of the gardening year.

PROTECTING SOIL IN WINTER

Winter weather can be quite damaging to exposed soil, which is why we aim to have all of our beds covered with a protective layer of mulch before winter really sets in. Straw can be used but there is another mulch material that is usually in ample supply at this time of the year: leaves. If they are dry, they might blow away when you put them down on your beds, so we keep them in place with something like a wire mesh until they start breaking down. If the leaves you gather are wet or already partially broken down, this will probably not be necessary. Another handy way to weigh down mulch material is with long stalks of plants such as corn or yacon. Under a blanket of mulch, the soil will remain loose and crumbly and next spring, the only thing you'll need to do is rake the mulch to the side before you can start sowing again.

LOOKING BACK AND EVALUATING

As I mentioned before, the garden plan I make at the beginning of the year inevitably undergoes a few changes as the season progresses, so at the end of the year I draw a new one that records what I really ended up sowing and planting in each bed. I also leaf through my garden diary in which I recorded sowing and planting times, harvests and failures. Every year I usually do a few experiments and it is good to sit down and evaluate what went well and what did not when the results are still fresh in my memory.

HARVESTING

Leeks, parsnips, Jerusalem artichokes, Brussels sprouts, kale, chard, winter purslane, corn salad, leaf mustard, radicchio.

SUBJECT INDEX

PLANT INDEX